大学英语拓展课程系列教材

新编体育英语

NEW SPORTS ENGLISH 1

总主编 杨小彬　主编 杨　柳
副主编 杨　慧　侯　润　卢　洁
编者　常　娟　熊召永　樊国刚　桂　滢
　　　黄　薇　夏少芳

清华大学出版社
北京

版权所有，侵权必究。举报：010-62782989，beiqinquan@tup.tsinghua.edu.cn。

图书在版编目（CIP）数据

新编体育英语.1 / 杨柳主编. —北京：清华大学出版社，2017（2023.8重印）
（大学英语拓展课程系列教材 / 杨小彬总主编）
ISBN 978-7-302-48276-5

Ⅰ.①新… Ⅱ.①杨… Ⅲ.①体育–英语–高等学校–教材 Ⅳ.①G8

中国版本图书馆CIP数据核字（2017）第207855号

责任编辑：曹诗悦
封面设计：平　原
责任校对：王凤芝
责任印制：沈　露

出版发行：清华大学出版社
网　　址：http://www.tup.com.cn, http://www.wqbook.com
地　　址：北京清华大学学研大厦A座　　邮　编：100084
社 总 机：010-83470000　　邮　购：010-62786544
投稿与读者服务：010-62776969, c-service@tup.tsinghua.edu.cn
质量反馈：010-62772015, zhiliang@tup.tsinghua.edu.cn

印 装 者：涿州市般润文化传播有限公司
经　　销：全国新华书店
开　　本：185mm×260mm　　印　张：8.25　　字　数：179千字
版　　次：2017年6月第1版　　印　次：2023年8月第6次印刷
定　　价：42.00元

产品编号：076953-02

⌘ 教材理念

　　高等教育国际化对大学英语教学提出了新的挑战和要求。2015 年颁布的《国务院关于印发统筹推进世界一流大学和一流学科建设总体方案的通知》（国发 [2015]64 号）要求，高校应"加强创新创业教育，大力推进个性化培养，全面提升学生的综合素质、国际视野、科学精神和创业意识、创造能力"。《国家中长期教育改革和发展规划纲要（2010—2020年）》明确指出，高校要"适应国家经济社会对外开放要求，培养大批具有国际视野、通晓国际规则、能够参与国际事务和国际竞争的国际化人才"。在教育国际化的背景下，高等教育的使命之一就是为国家培养国际化人才，这其中，大学英语教学肩负着重要使命。

　　然而，国内部分高校对于大学英语教学的定位并不明确，盲目强调四、六级英语证书的重要性，忽视学生专业发展的个性需求，从而导致学生大学英语学习积极性不高，课堂教学缺乏有效性。这在体育专业学生身上表现尤为突出。目前，随着体育文化交流与体育赛事日趋国际化，体育英语的重要性日益凸显。除了部分体育专业院校开设有专业英语课程外，多数综合性大学的体育专业仍遵循传统的通用英语教学模式，缺乏渗透体育元素的专业英语熏陶。因此，有必要转变教学观念，在提高体育专业学生英语水平的基础上，融入一些体育英语知识，以提高体育专业学生大学英语课程学习的有效性和实用性。

　　本教材目标定位介于"通用英语"和"专门用途英语"之间，旨在帮助体育专业学生用英语获取专业领域知识，提高其语言应用能力，以适应未来职业发展的需要。具体来说，本教材希望提高学生的语言表达能力、语篇层次上的阅读能力、体育专业英语术语的翻译和理解能力，为他们将来从事体育教育、体育外事、体育新闻、体育研究和体育网络编辑等工作打下良好的基础。

⌘ 教材特色

　　本教材在设计过程中从主题内容、活动练习、知识体系等多方面进行精心策划，呈现以下特点：

1. 精心选材，内容新颖

　　本教材综合了体育学科下各专业特点，涉及体育教育、社会体育、休闲体育以及运动体育科学等专业，视角多元，内容丰富。所选素材来源于国外网站最新的赛事规则、国际体育大会资料、技术手册以及国内外体育新闻报道和媒体评论等。教材编写时既考虑体育英语的原汁原味，又兼顾学生的语言实际水平，确保趣味性与实用性统一。

2. 科学编排，侧重实用

本教材针对体育相关专业学生的英语学习需求，加强语言技能训练，同时侧重于对外体育交往中的实际应用，将日常生活与体育交往的不同场景交融在一起，真正培养学生的英语应用能力。

⌘ 教材框架

每单元的基本结构为：

第一部分：知识准备（Knowledge Preparation）。单元阅读学习的准备部分，主要提供本单元体育运动相关的概念、竞技规则或者文化背景知识等，帮助学生加深对单元体育运动的了解，完善其知识结构。

第二部分：阅读（Reading）。包括两篇主题课文，分别配有词汇和短语表以及相关练习。Text A 为精读课文，建议教师精讲精练；Text B 是对本单元话题的扩展或深化，目的在于开拓学生思路。练习活动丰富：课文理解题型包括文章框架图、细节多选题和对错判断等，注重引导学生在具体语境中学习专业知识，抓住关键信息，培养其归纳和演绎能力；词汇练习注重考察在语境中理解词义，练习所用语料均为原文原句，有相对完整的语境，学生在做练习的同时进一步巩固原汁原味的语言表达；文中重难点句子的英汉互译练习，进一步训练学生的翻译能力。

第三部分：听说（Listening and Speaking）。根据单元主题设计两道练习题目。第一道为情景对话，第二道为短文理解。听说部分既有听前活动的热身，又有判断对错与多项选择等形式的理解练习，并配有词汇表。

第四部分：写作（Writing）。鼓励学生参照范例写作，写作文体涉及信函、个人简历、入学申请、参会表格等实用性应用文体。

本教材内容安排灵活，教师可以根据授课计划、学生英语水平和专业特点，自主选取教学内容，因材施教，以培养学生英语应用能力、自主学习能力和体育文化素养。教材配有听力音频、电子课件、习题参考答案等教学资源，广大教师可下载参考*。

本教材编者团队为大学英语一线教师，均有教授体育专业学生大学英语课程的教学经历。教材编写分工如下：听力部分：侯润；写作部分：常娟；阅读部分：熊召永（Unit 1）、樊国刚（Unit 2）、杨慧（Unit 3）、桂滢（Unit 4）、夏少芳（Unit 5）、黄薇（Unit 6）、杨柳（Unit 7）、卢洁（Unit 8）。此外，本教材还有一支顾问团队，他们是具有国内外体育大赛裁判和体育教学经历且理论功底深厚的体育教师们，他们为教材的知识框架建立提供了有力的专业保障。编写团队和顾问团队的合作确保了教材内容的准确性、语言的地道性和任务的真实性，保证了教材的质量。尽管如此，由于教材涉及大量体育专业知识，编者编写水平有限，书中不当之处在所难免，请各位专家和广大读者批评指正。

编者
2017 年 5 月于武汉

---

* 请登录 www.tsinghuaelt.com 下载。

Contents

Unit 1　Football
足球 1

- Text A　Exploring FIFA......3
- Text B　Exploring Football Culture......8

Unit 2　Basketball
篮球 17

- Text A　Kareem Abdul-Jabbar......19
- Text B　NBA All-Star Game......26

Unit 3　Race Walking
竞走 33

- Text A　Race Walking......35
- Text B　Race Walking vs. Power Walking......39

Unit 4　Recreational Sports
休闲体育 45

- Text A　Sport Climbing......46
- Text B　The World's Craziest Crazy Golf Course?......52

Unit 5　Chinese Traditional Sports
中国传统体育 59

- Text A　Bruce Lee and His Martial Arts......61
- Text B　Magic Taijiquan......67

Unit 6　Sports Culture
体育文化 75

- Text A　Olympic Gold Medals or Olympic Spirit?......77
- Text B　China's Traditional Sports Culture......82

Unit 7　Sports Science
体育科学 89

- Text A　Physical Literacy: Teaching Children the ABCs of Movement......91
- Text B　Fruits & Veggies—Do You Eat Too Few? 96

Unit 8　International Referees
国际裁判 103

- Text A　FIVB Beach Volleyball......104
- Text B　Volleyball Comes Home to Copacabana 110

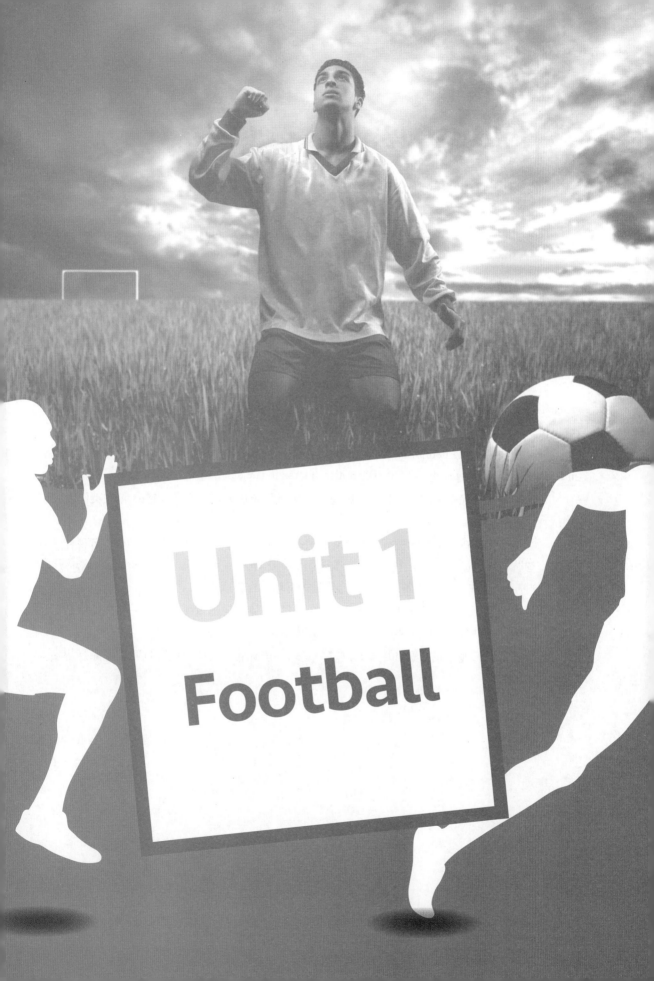

Unit 1
Football

Part One Knowledge Preparation

Football originated from a ball game called "cuju" in ancient China, and after being spread to Europe by Arabs, it developed into "modern football" in Britain in 1863.

A football game is played between two teams, each attempting to win by scoring more goals than their opponent. Each team has eleven players and three substitutes, or reserve players. The team consists of a goalkeeper, defenders, midfield players, and forwards (or strikers). A game of football is split into two halves of 45 minutes each, with a 15-minute break at halftime. A referee and two assistants make sure that nobody cheats or breaks the rules.

Football is played predominantly with the feet, but players may use any part of their body except their hands and arms to propel the ball; the exceptions are the two goalkeepers, who are the only players allowed to handle the ball in the field of play, albeit with restrictions.

Football is played both at an amateur level and professional level all over the world. The international governing body is FIFA (Fédération Internationale de Football Association).

足球起源于古代中国的球类运动"蹴鞠",后经阿拉伯人传入欧洲,1863年在英国发展成现代足球。

一场足球比赛在两队之间进行,以比对方进球多为胜。每队11人,另外还有3名替补球员。球队由守门员、后卫、中场球员、前锋组成。比赛分上下半场,各45分钟,中场休息15分钟。一名主裁判和两名助理裁判监督是否有球员作弊或犯规。

球员主要用脚踢球,除了手和手臂以外,可以用身体任何部位触球。唯一的例外就是守门员,他们可以在场内用手触球,虽然有一定限制。

世界各地都有业余足球赛和职业足球赛。足球的国际管理机构是国际足联(国际足协联合会)。

Part Two   Reading

Exploring FIFA

1. The Fédération Internationale de Football Association (FIFA), called "International Federation of Association Football", is the international governing body of association football, futsal, and beach soccer. FIFA is responsible for the organization of football's major international tournaments, notably the World Cup which commenced in 1930 in Uruguay, and the Women's World Cup which started in 1991 in China.

2. FIFA was founded in 1904 to oversee international competitions among the national associations of Belgium, Denmark, France, Germany, the Netherlands, Spain, Sweden, and Switzerland. Headquartered in Zürich, its membership now comprises 211 national associations. Each member country should also be the member of one of the six regional confederations: Africa, Asia, Europe, North & Central America and the Caribbean, Oceania, and South America.

3. Although FIFA does not control the rules of football (that being the responsibility of the International Football Association Board), it is responsible for both the organization of a number of tournaments and their promotion, which generate revenue from sponsorship. In 2013, FIFA had revenues of over 1.3 billion U.S. dollars, for a net profit of 72 million U.S. dollars, and had cash reserves of over 1.4 billion U.S. dollars.

4. FIFA's supreme body is the FIFA Congress, made up of representatives from each affiliated member association. Each national football association has one vote, regardless of its size or footballing strength. The Congress assembles in ordinary session once every year, and extraordinary sessions have been held once a year since 1998. The Congress makes decisions relating to FIFA's governing statutes and their method of implementation and application. Only the Congress can pass changes to FIFA's statutes. The Congress approves the annual report, and decides on the acceptance of new national associations and holds elections. The Congress elects the President of FIFA, its General Secretary, and the other members of the FIFA Council on the year following the FIFA World Cup.

5. FIFA's Executive Committee, chaired by the President, is the main decision-making body of the organization in the intervals of the Congress. The Executive Committee is composed of

25 people: the President, eight Vice Presidents, and 15 members and one woman member. The Executive Committee is the body that decides which country will host the World Cup.

6 The President and the General Secretary are the main officeholders of FIFA, and are in charge of its daily administration. Gianni Infantino is the current president, appointed on 26 February 2016 at the Extraordinary FIFA Congress.

7 FIFA is the most important international football organization, whose aim is not only to improve and promote football and organize exciting tournaments around the world, but also to care about the society and environment and pay much attention to fighting corruption.

Word Bank

tournament	['tʊrnəmənt]	n. 比赛；锦标赛
notably	['noʊtəbli]	adv. 显著地；尤其
commence	[kə'mens]	v. 开始；着手
oversee	[ˌoʊvər'siː]	v. 监督；审查
headquarter	['hed'kwɔːtə]	v. 在……设总部
comprise	[kəm'praɪz]	v. 包含，由……组成
regional	['riːdʒənl]	adj. 地区的；局部的
promotion	[prə'moʊʃn]	n. 推广，晋升；推销，促销；促进；发扬，振兴
generate	['dʒenəreɪt]	v. 生成，产生，发生
revenue	['revənuː]	n. 税收，国家的收入；收益
sponsorship	['spɑːnsərʃɪp]	n. 赞助；发起
reserve	[rɪ'zɜːrv]	n. 储备，储存；自然保护区
supreme	[suː'priːm]	adj. 最高的，至高的；最重要的
session	['seʃn]	n. 会议
affiliated	[ə'fɪlieɪtɪd]	adj. 附属的；有关联的
assemble	[ə'sembl]	v. 集合，聚集
statute	['stætʃuːt]	n. 章程；法规，法令；条例
implementation	[ˌɪmplɪmen'teɪʃn]	n. 执行，履行；实现
interval	['ɪntərvl]	n. 间隔，间距；幕间休息
host	[hoʊst]	v. 主持；当主人招待
administration	[ədˌmɪnɪ'streɪʃn]	n. 管理；行政；实施；行政机构
appoint	[ə'pɔɪnt]	v. 任命，指定；约定
corruption	[kə'rʌpʃn]	n. 贪污，腐败；堕落

Phrases

net profit	纯利润
regardless of	不管，不顾，不论
decide on	决定，选定
be composed of	由……组成
in charge of	负责，掌管

Proper Names

FIFA	国际足联
World Cup	国际足联世界杯（与奥运会并称为全球体育两大最顶级赛事）
futsal	室内五人制足球（起源于加拿大）
beach soccer	沙滩足球
the Caribbean	加勒比海地区
International Football Association Board	国际足协理事会
FIFA Congress	国际足联代表大会
FIFA Council	国际足联理事会
FIFA's Executive Committee	国际足联执行委员会
Gianni Infantino	詹尼·因凡蒂诺（现任国际足联主席）

Task 1 Text Organization

Read the text and fill in the blanks.

Paragraphs	Key Words	Supporting Details
Beginning (Para. 1)	The _____	• an international governing body of association football, _____ and _____ • responsible for the international major tournaments notably (1) _____ (2) _____

Body (Paras. 2–6)	Further introduction	• birth: (1) founded in _____ (2) headquartered in _____ (3) oversaw the international competitions among _____ national associations • membership now: (1) _____ national associations (2) _____ regional confederations • revenues in 2013: (1) from _____ (2) _____ U.S. dollars for a _____ profit of 72 million U.S. dollars, and cash _____ of 1.4 billion U.S. dollars.
End (Para. 7)	The most important international football organization	• its aim is to: (1) _____ and _____ football (2) _____ exciting tournaments around the world (3) care about the _____ and _____ (4) pay much attention to fighting _____

Task 2 Reading Comprehension

Exercise 1

Read the text and decide whether the following statements are true (T) or false (F).

1. _____ FIFA is the international governing body of association football, futsal, and street soccer.
2. _____ The six regional football confederations are: Africa, Asia, Europe, Oceania, South America and North America.
3. _____ The first Women's World Cup commenced in 1991 in China.
4. _____ Only the Congress can pass changes to FIFA's statutes.
5. _____ FIFA does not control the rules of football.

Exercise 2

Read the text and answer the following questions.

1. What does FIFA stand for? What kind of organization is it?

2. Which body of FIFA elects its President? What is it made up of?
3. Which body of FIFA decides the host country of the World Cup? What is it composed of?
4. Who is the current President of FIFA? When was he appointed?

Task 3 Language in Use

Exercise 1

Match the underlined words in the left column with their corresponding meanings in the right column.

1. FIFA is responsible for the organization of football's major international tournaments, <u>notably</u> the World Cup.

   A. gather together

2. Headquartered in Zürich, its membership now <u>comprises</u> 211 national associations.

   B. the act of carrying out a plan, policy, etc.

3. It is responsible for both the organization of a number of tournaments and their promotion, which generate revenue from <u>sponsorship</u>.

   C. highest in position, especially of power

4. FIFA's <u>supreme</u> body is the FIFA Congress, made up of representatives from each affiliated member association.

   D. financial support for an event or activity

5. The Congress <u>assembles</u> in ordinary session once every year, and extraordinary sessions have been held once a year since 1998.

   E. activities or work such as managing and organizing affairs in an institution, company, etc.

6. The Congress makes decisions relating to FIFA's governing statutes and their method of <u>implementation</u> and application.

   F. consist of, include

7. The President and the General Secretary are the main officeholders of FIFA, and are in charge of its daily <u>administration</u>.

   G. especially or particularly

Exercise 2

Select one word or phrase for each blank from a list of choices given below.

| regardless of | statues | following | affiliated | annual |
| decides on | relating to | implementation | sessions | supreme |

FIFA's 1._____ body is the FIFA Congress, made up of representatives from each 2._____ member association. Each national football association has one vote, 3._____ its size or footballing strength. The Congress assembles in ordinary session once every year, and extraordinary 4._____ have been held once a year since 1998. The Congress makes decisions 5._____ FIFA's governing statutes and their method of 6._____ and application. Only the Congress can pass changes to FIFA's 7._____. The Congress approves the 8._____ report and 9._____ the acceptance of new national associations and holds elections. The Congress elects the President of FIFA, its General Secretary, and the other members of the FIFA Council on the year 10._____ the FIFA World Cup.

 Exercise 3

Translate the following sentences into English.
1. 大卫负责球队的日常管理。(be in charge of)
2. 我们已经选定了比赛日期。(decide on)
3. 每队由 11 名球员组成，包括守门员、后卫、中场球员和前锋。(be composed of)
4. 每个国家协会不论其大小或足球实力都有一张选票。(regardless of)

Text B

Exploring Football Culture

Football culture refers to the cultural aspects surrounding the game of association football. In many countries, football has ingrained itself into the national culture, and parts of life may revolve around it. Many countries have daily football newspapers, as well as football magazines. Football players, especially in the top levels of the game, have become role models for ordinary people. The FIFA World Cup held every four years is the quintessential football event, combining the greatest players in the world and the passion of the fans. Football has a long and glorious history, with which a vast and diverse culture has emerged.

Fair Play

Fair Play is the name of a FIFA program which aims to increase sportsmanship as well as prevent discrimination in the game of football. This also involves programs to reduce racism in the game. The program extends to outside of football, in trying to support charities and other organizations which improve conditions around the world.

Rivalries

Derby matches, which are matches between two neighboring rival clubs, are often fiercely competitive. Sometimes there are underlying political or sectarian tensions. The term often applies to matches between two teams from the same city or region, but it is sometimes used to refer to matches between big clubs from the same country. Derbies are usually treated as the most important matches by the fans, players and clubs.

Celebrities

Such is the popularity of football that some players become better known for their "off-the-pitch" activities. The celebrity status is such that advertisers and sports goods manufacturers hire them to sponsor their products.

The English footballer David Beckham has been perceived as a trend-setter in England due to a history of frequent hairstyle changes. Beckham was for a long time an Armani model, famous for his underwear advertisements. In late-2009 Beckham was replaced by the Portuguese midfielder Cristiano Ronaldo as Armani's primary footballer model.

Globalization

In the modern game most clubs have multiple foreign players; this is especially evident in the English Premier League where English players are outnumbered by their foreign counterparts. Many teams attempt to build a complete team with players with ball control, others with strength, others with speed and others with vision. Traditionally these skill sets are associated with different regions; ball control is regarded as a South American trait, speed is typically associated with African players and strength is typically seen as the European way. Football has become a global sport where spectators from around the world can enjoy many different leagues.

Coaches are also becoming sought after internationally. This extends to national team coaches, once being native to their country, being brought in from other countries. Dutch coach Guus Hiddink has an iconic status in South Korea after coaching its national team to the semifinals of the 2002 World Cup. So much so that one of South Korea's World Cup stadiums was renamed in his honor shortly after the competition. The famous Italian "Silver Fox" Marcello Lippi became the head coach of the Chinese team after his success in Guangzhou Evergrand.

Word Bank

quintessential	[ˌkwɪntɪˈsenʃl]	adj. 精髓的，精粹的
passion	[ˈpæʃn]	n. 激情；热情；酷爱
diverse	[daɪˈvɜːrs]	adj. 不同的；多种多样的
emerge	[iˈmɜːrdʒ]	v. 出现，显现，浮现
sportsmanship	[ˈspɔːrtsmənʃɪp]	n. 运动风范，体育道德
discrimination	[dɪˌskrɪmɪˈneɪʃn]	n. 歧视

racism	['reɪsɪzəm]	n. 种族主义，种族歧视；人种偏见
charity	['tʃærəti]	n. 慈善；施舍；慈善团体
rivalry	['raɪvlri]	n. 对抗，较劲
fiercely	['fɪrsli]	adv. 猛烈地，激烈地
underlying	[ˌʌndər'laɪɪŋ]	adj. 潜在的；根本的
sectarian	[sek'teriən]	adj. 宗派的
celebrity	[sə'lebrəti]	n. 名人
pitch	[pɪtʃ]	n. 足球场
globalization	[ˌgloʊbələ'zeɪʃn]	n. 全球化
outnumber	[ˌaʊt'nʌmbər]	v. 数目超过；比……多
counterpart	['kaʊntərpɑːrt]	n. 对应的人或物
trait	[treɪt]	n. 特性，特点；品质
iconic	[aɪ'kɑːnɪk]	adj. 偶像的；图标的
coach	[koʊtʃ]	n. 教练 v. 训练，执教

Phrases

ingrain... into...	使……根深蒂固于
revolve around	围绕，以……为中心
apply to	适用于
perceive... as...	认为……是……
be associated with	和……联系在一起，与……有关
seek after	寻找，追寻
in one's honor	向……表示致敬

Proper Names

fair play	公平竞赛
Derby	同城德比，国家德比
English Premier League	英格兰足球超级联赛
David Beckham	大卫·贝克汉姆
Armani	阿玛尼（世界著名时装品牌）
Cristiano Ronaldo	克里斯蒂亚诺·罗纳尔多
Guus Hiddink	胡斯·希丁克
Marcello Lippi	马尔切洛·里皮
Guangzhou Evergrand	广州恒大

Unit 1
Football

Critical Reading and Thinking

Read the text and decide whether the following statements are true (T) or false (F).

1. _____ Football culture is concerned with the cultural aspects surrounding the game of association football.
2. _____ Football players, especially in the mid-levels of the game, have become role models for people.
3. _____ The FIFA World Cup held every three years is the quintessential football event, combining the greatest players in the world and the passion of the fans.
4. _____ Fair Play only refers to increasing sportsmanship and preventing discrimination in the game of football.
5. _____ Football celebrities are so popular that advertisers and sports goods manufacturers hire them to sponsor their products.
6. _____ Derby matches refer to matches between two teams from the same city or region or matches between big clubs from the same country.
7. _____ The English football player David Beckham has been regarded as a trend-setter in England because of frequent hairstyle changes.
8. _____ In late-2009 the Brazilian midfielder Cristiano Ronaldo took the place of Beckham as Armani's primary footballer model.
9. _____ There are more foreign players than native players in the Italian Premier League.
10. _____ The South Korean team was led by Dutch coach Guus Hiddink to the semifinals of the 2002 World Cup.

Translation

Translate the following sentences into Chinese.

1. In many countries, football has ingrained itself into the national culture, and parts of life may revolve around it.
2. Derby matches, which are matches between two neighboring rival clubs, are often fiercely competitive. Sometimes there are underlying political or sectarian tensions.
3. The FIFA World Cup held every four years is the quintessential football event, combining the greatest players in the world and the passion of the fans.
4. Traditionally these skill sets are associated with different regions; ball control is regarded as a South American trait, speed is typically associated with African players and strength is typically seen as the European way.
5. Coaches are also becoming sought after internationally. This extends to national team coaches, once being native to their country, being brought in from other countries.

Part Three — Listening and Speaking

Task 1

Word Bank

gifted	['gɪftɪd]	adj. 有天赋的，有才华的
fantastic	[fæn'tæstɪk]	adj. 极好的
submit	[səb'mɪt]	v. 提交
application	[ˌæplɪ'keɪʃn]	n. 应用；申请
tryout	['traɪaʊt]	n. 挑选，选拔
FC Barcelona		巴塞罗那足球俱乐部
Lionel Messi		里奥·梅西（足球明星）

Listen to a conversation between two students talking about football and answer the following questions.

1. Where did Lee play football everyday when he was a kid?
2. Who is their favorite football player?
3. How often does Lee play football now?
4. How can they join the university's football team?
5. Where can they get the application form?

Task 2

Word Bank

prestigious	[pre'stɪdʒəs]	adj. 有名望的，享有声望的
govern	['gʌvərn]	v. 管理；支配
phase	[feɪz]	n. 阶段
qualification	[ˌkwɑːlɪfɪ'keɪʃn]	n. 资格；条件
continental	[ˌkɑːntɪ'nentl]	adj. 大陆的
championship	['tʃæmpiənʃɪp]	n. 锦标赛；冠军称号
enormous	[ɪ'nɔːrməs]	adj. 巨大的
Argentina	[ˌɑːrdʒən'tiːnə]	n. 阿根廷（拉丁美洲国家）
Uruguay	['jʊrəgwaɪ]	n. 乌拉圭（拉丁美洲国家）

Unit 1
Football

Listen to a passage about the FIFA World Cup and choose the best answer to each question.

1. In which year was the World Cup first held?
   A. 1913. **B.** 1930. **C.** 1942. **D.** 1946.
2. How many teams compete in the World Cup Finals?
   A. 20. **B.** 22. **C.** 32. **D.** 36.
3. What country has NOT won the World Cup championship?
   A. England. **B.** France.
   C. Uruguay. **D.** the Netherlands.
4. What country will host the 2018 World Cup?
   A. Spain. **B.** Russia.
   C. Brazil. **D.** Italy.

Task 3

Listen to the five sentences from the recording, repeat each sentence after it is spoken, and then write them down.

1. _____.
2. _____.
3. _____.
4. _____.
5. _____.

Part Four — Writing

Forms

Forms are frequently used by official and business organizations to collect one's personal information for various purposes. There are registration forms, application forms, ticket reservation forms and so on. They may be presented traditionally in paper, or put up online electronically. The basic information requested is mostly personal details. Some forms may only include several items (see Sample 1) while others may require many more details (see Sample 2). Remember, you have to make sure all the information is correct while filling in such forms.

Sample 1　Online registration form

First name*

Last name or initial*

Email address*

Choose a password (min. 8 characters)*

Please make sure your email address is correct so we can get in touch with you.

Register

By clicking Register I agree to Futurelearn's Terms & Conditions and Privacy Policy, and I agree to abide by the Code of Conduct.

Sample 2　Application form of scholarship for international young scientists

Applicant's information					
Surname	*Cheng*	Middle name		Given name	*Xiang*
Gender	*Male*	Date of birth	*July 23, 1970*	Nationality	*Chinese*
Highest academic degree		*Doctor's Degree of Kinesiology*			
Current employer (if any)		*Shanghai University of Sport*			
Current position (if any)					
Contact information in your country					

Office

School of Sport Science,

Shanghai University of Sport,

399 Chang Hai Road,

Shanghai, 200438,

P. R. China

Tel: +86 21 51257246

Home

533 QingYuan Ring Rd.,

Shanghai 200438,

P. R. China

Tel: +86 21 51253699

Host institution's information

Host institution	The Australian National University		
Address	The Australian National University, Canberra	Postal Code	2600
Host researcher	William Hamilton	E-mail	internationaloffice@anu.edu.au
Tel.	+61 2 6125 4321	Fax	+61 2 6125 1234

Follow-up Writing

Fill in the following registration form to join Apollo DB City Club.

MEMBERSHIP APPLICATION FORM

Date: ....

The Manager,
Apollo DB City Club, Indore

Dear Sir,
I want to use the services of The Apollo DB City Club.

Name: _____

Father's Name/Husband's Name: _____

_____

Nationality: _____

Residence Address: _____ Office Address: _____

Phone: _____ Phone: _____
Mobile NO.: _____ Mobile NO.: _____
E-mail: _____

All mail to be sent on: Residence Address ☐   Office Address ☐

My membership is being proposed by the following two club members of the Apollo DB City.

Name: _____   Name: _____

Signature: _____   Signature: _____

Mobile NO.: _____ Tel. _____   Mobile NO.: _____ Tel. _____

We agree to abide by the rules and regulations of the Apollo DB City club that may be in force from time to time and pay all the dues as applicable from time to time. We also agree that my membership may be terminated immediately if the Apollo DB City club management concludes that I/we or my/our family members or our guests have violated any club's rules, regulation, general instructions and failed to maintain the club decorum as well as failed to clear the maintenance charges or other dues in time.

Part One Knowledge Preparation

Basketball originated in the United States. It was first invented in December 1891 by Dr. James Naismith, a teacher at the International Young Men's Christian Association Training School (today, Springfield College) in Springfield, Massachusetts. At that time, his superior asked him to come up with an indoor game that could be played during the winter months. He wrote the basic rules and nailed two peach baskets onto a ten-foot (3.05 m) elevated track near the roof. The peach baskets were used until 1906 when they were finally replaced by metal hoops with backboards. A further change was soon made, so the ball merely passed through. Whenever a person got the ball in the basket, his team would gain a point. Whichever team got the most points won the game.

There are many techniques for ball-handling—shooting, passing, dribbling and rebounding. Basketball teams generally have player positions. The tallest and strongest members of a team are called center or power forward, while slightly shorter and more agile players are called small forward, and the shortest players or those who possess the best ball-handling skills are called point guard or shooting guard. The point guard directs the on-court action, implementing the coach's game plan, and managing the execution of offensive and defensive plays.

Basketball is one of the world's most popular and widely viewed sports. The National Basketball Association (NBA) is the most popular and widely considered to be the highest level of professional basketball in the world.

篮球运动起源于美国。1891年12月，美国马萨诸塞州斯普林菲尔德市基督教青年会训练学校（今斯普林菲尔德学院）体育教师詹姆士·奈史密斯博士发明了篮球。当时他的上级让他设计一项能够在寒冷的冬季开展的室内运动。他制订了篮球的基本规则，并将两只桃篮分别钉在靠近屋顶的10英尺（3.05米）高的两端看台的栏杆上。直到1906年桃篮才最终被带篮板的金属篮筐取代。后来人们又对篮筐作了改进，让球能直接穿过。当一名队员把球投进篮筐，他所在的队伍就得1分。得分多的球队获胜。

篮球技术包括投篮、传球、运球和篮板球。队员通常都有位置分工。队中身材最高最壮的队员出任中锋或大前锋，而身高稍矮、更为敏捷的队员担任小前锋，身高最矮或控球技术最好的队员充当控球后卫或得分后卫。控球后卫主导场上比赛，执行教练的战术意图，并掌控全队的攻防节奏。

篮球是世界上观赏人数最多、最受大众喜爱的运动项目之一。美国职业篮球联赛（NBA）是公认的最高水准的篮球比赛，深受观众喜爱。

Part Two Reading

Text A

Kareem Abdul-Jabbar

Full Name: Kareem Abdul-Jabbar
Formerly known as: Ferdinand Lewis Alcindor
Born: 4/16/1947 in New York
High School: Power Memorial (N.Y.)
College: UCLA
Drafted by: Milwaukee Bucks (first overall pick in 1969)
Transactions: Traded to Los Angeles Lakers, 6/16/1975
Height: 7 ft 2 in (2.18 m)
Weight: 267 lbs. (121 kg)
Honors: Naismith Memorial Basketball Hall of Fame (1995); NBA champion (1971, 1980, 1982, 1985, 1987, 1988); NBA MVP (1971, 1972, 1974, 1976, 1977, 1980); 10-time All-NBA First Team; Five-time All-NBA Second Team; Five-time All-Defensive First Team; Six-time All-Defensive Second Team; 19-time All-Star; One of the 50 Greatest Players in NBA History (1996).

1 When Kareem Abdul-Jabbar left the game in 1989 at age 42, no NBA player had ever scored more points, blocked more shots, won more Most Valuable Player Awards, played in more All-Star Games or logged more seasons. His list of personal and team accomplishments is perhaps the most awesome in league history: Rookie of the Year, member of six NBA championship teams, six-time NBA MVP, two-time NBA Finals MVP, 19-time All-Star, two-time scoring champion, and a member of the NBA 35th and 50th Anniversary All-Time Teams. He also owned eight playoff records and seven All-Star records. No player achieved as much individual and team success as Abdul-Jabbar did.

2 Players 10 years younger couldn't keep up with Abdul-Jabbar, whose strict physical-fitness regimen was years ahead of its time in the NBA. But if others have since emulated his fitness regimen, no player has ever duplicated his trademark "sky-hook". Although labeled "unsexy" by Abdul-Jabbar himself, the shot became one of the most effective weapons in all of sports. An all-around player, Abdul-Jabbar brought grace, agility, and versatility to the center position, which had previously been characterized solely by power and size.

3 Abdul-Jabbar was born Ferdinand Lewis Alcindor Jr. in New York City in 1947. He was the only child of an overprotective mother and a strict father. As the tallest kid in the Harlem school system, Alcindor was viewed as something of a freak by his schoolmates. After dominating New York high school basketball at Power Memorial, he enrolled at UCLA and played for John Wooden's powerhouse Bruins.

4 Alcindor simply ruled the college ranks. He was selected as Player of the Year in 1967 and 1969. He was also named an All-American and the most outstanding player in the NCAA Tournament in 1967, 1968 and 1969. With Alcindor taking charge in the middle, Wooden and UCLA won three NCAA championships.

5 The Milwaukee Bucks made Alcindor the first overall choice in the 1969 NBA Draft. With Alcindor aboard in 1969–1970, the Bucks rose to second place in the Eastern Division. Alcindor was an instant star, placing second in the league in scoring (28.8 ppg) and third in rebounding (14.5 rpg). He easily won the NBA Rookie of the Year honor.

6 Before the 1971–1972 season Alcindor converted from Catholicism to Islam and took the name Kareem Abdul-Jabbar, which means "noble, powerful servant". He was certainly a noble, powerful player. In 1971–1972 he repeated as scoring champion (34.8 ppg) and NBA Most Valuable Player, and the Bucks repeated as division leaders.

7 Despite his success in Milwaukee, Abdul-Jabbar was unhappy due to the lack of people who shared his religious and cultural beliefs and wanted out. He requested that he be traded to either New York or Los Angeles, and Bucks General Manager Wayne Embry complied, sending Abdul-Jabbar to the Lakers in 1975. The second Abdul-Jabbar dynasty was about to take shape.

8 In 1979, the Lakers selected a 6-foot-9-point guard named Earvin "Magic" Johnson from Michigan State. Johnson's arrival marked the beginning of a decade that would bring Abdul-Jabbar five more championship rings. With a fast break that came to be known as "Showtime", the Lakers won nine division titles in the final 10 years of Abdul-Jabbar's career. The Lakers reached the NBA Finals eight times in the 10 seasons between 1979–1980 and 1988–1989. They won five NBA championships.

9 Abdul-Jabbar's retirement marked the end of an era for the NBA. He left the game as its all-time scorer, which may never be surpassed, with 38,387 points (24.6 ppg), 17,440 rebounds (11.2 rpg), 3,189 blocks, and a 0.559 field-goal percentage from a career that spanned 20 years

and 1,560 games. He scored in double figures in 787 straight games. Since retiring, Abdul-Jabbar has authored several books, worked in the entertainment business and served as a "basketball ambassador", working in various capacities such as a coach and broadcaster as well as helped to fight hunger and illiteracy. In 1995, Abdul-Jabbar was elected to the Naismith Memorial Basketball Hall of Fame.

Word Bank

block	[blɑːk]	v. 阻止；阻塞；限制；封盖
awesome	['ɔːsəm]	adj. 令人敬畏的；可怕的；极好的
rookie	['rʊki]	n. 新手，新人
playoff	['pleɪɔːf]	n. 季后赛；复赛
regimen	['redʒɪmən]	n. [医] 养生法；生活规则；政体
emulate	['emjuleɪt]	v. 模仿，效仿
duplicate	['duːplɪkeɪt]	v. 复制；使加倍
sky-hook	[skai-huk]	n. 天钩；大钩手
label	['leɪbl]	v. 贴标签于；标注
all-around	[ˌɔːl əˈraʊnd]	adj. 全面的；综合性的
agility	[əˈdʒɪləti]	n. 敏捷，灵活；机敏
versatility	[ˌvɜːrsəˈtɪləti]	n. 多才多艺；用途广泛
freak	[friːk]	n. 怪人；怪事
division	[dɪˈvɪʒn]	n. [体] 赛区；除法；部门；分割
Catholicism	[kəˈθɑːləsɪzəm]	n. 天主教
Islam	[ˈɪzlɑːm]	n. 伊斯兰教
comply	[kəmˈplaɪ]	v. 遵守，顺从，遵从；答应
surpass	[sərˈpæs]	v. 超越；胜过，优于
span	[spæn]	v. 跨越；持续
ambassador	[æmˈbæsədər]	n. 大使；代表；使节
illiteracy	[ɪˈlɪtərəsi]	n. 文盲；无知

Phrases

be characterized by	具有……的特性；以……为特征
ppg. (points per game)	场均得分
rpg. (rebounds per game)	场均篮板数
convert to	转换成
take shape	形成；成形
fast break	快攻

field-goal percentage	投篮命中率；投球命中率
double figures	两位数（10~99）

Proper Names

Kareem Abdul-Jabbar	卡里姆·阿卜杜尔·贾巴尔（篮球球星）
Most Valuable Player Award	最有价值球员奖
Rookie of the Year	年度最佳新秀
NBA Finals MVP	NBA 总决赛最有价值球员
Power Memorial	能量纪念馆中学（纽约）
powerhouse Bruins	大棕熊队（篮球队名）
Player of the Year	年度最佳球员
NCAA Tournament	全美大学生篮球锦标赛
NBA Draft	NBA 选秀
Naismith Memorial Basketball Hall of Fame	奈史密斯篮球名人堂

Task 1 Text Organization

Read the text and fill in the blanks.

Paragraphs	Key Words	Supporting Details
Beginning (Paras. 1–2)	General description of Kareem Abdul-Jabbar	• Kareem Abdul-Jabbar retired in 1989 at age _____, he scored the most _____, blocked the most _____, won the most MVP _____, played in more _____ Games or logged the most _____ in the NBA. • His list of personal and team accomplishments is perhaps the most _____ in league history. • He had a unique physical-fitness _____ and brought _____, _____, and versatility to the center position, which had previously been characterized solely by _____ and _____.

Unit 2
Basketball

Body (Paras. 3–8)	His basketball career	• Being the tallest kid in the Harlem school system, he dominated New York _____ _____ basketball and later he enrolled at _____. • He simply ruled the _____ ranks and helped his team win _____ national championships. • When he played for the Milwaukee Bucks for the first year, he easily won the NBA _____ of the Year honor. • In 1971–1972 he repeated as scoring _____ (34.8 ppg) and NBA Most Valuable Player, and the Bucks repeated as _____ leaders. • In 1975, he was traded from the Milwaukee Bucks to the Los Angeles _____. The second Abdul-Jabbar _____ was about to take shape. • The Lakers reached the NBA Finals _____ times in 10 seasons. They won _____ NBA championships.
End (Para. 9)	His retirement	• Since retiring, Abdul-Jabbar has authored several _____, worked in the entertainment business and served as a "basketball _____", working in various capacities such as a coach and broadcaster as well as helped to fight _____ and illiteracy. • In _____, Abdul-Jabbar was elected to the Naismith Memorial Basketball Hall of Fame.

Task 2 Reading Comprehension

Exercise 1

Read the text and decide whether the following statements are true (T) or false (F).

1. _____ When Kareem Abdul-Jabbar retired from the NBA, he was already 40 years old.
2. _____ Abdul-Jabbar has brought many changes to the center position.
3. _____ Abdul-Jabbar was very successful in Milwaukee and was happy to stay there.
4. _____ All together he has won six NBA championships, one in Milwaukee, the other five in Los Angeles.
5. _____ His NBA career lasted for 20 years.

Exercise 2

Read the text and answer the following questions.

1. At what age did Abdul-Jabbar enter the NBA league?
2. What did he think of his trademark "sky-hook"?
3. What was his former name before he became a Muslim?
4. Why did he want to leave the Milwaukee Bucks?
5. What did he do after retirement?

Task 3 Language in Use

Exercise 1

Match the underlined words or phrases in the left column with their corresponding meanings in the right column.

1. No NBA player had ever scored more points, <u>blocked</u> more shots, played in more All-Star Games than him.

   A. the gracefulness of a person or animal that is quick and alert

2. His list of personal and team accomplishments is perhaps the most <u>awesome</u> in league history.

   B. prevent the progress or accomplishment of

3. No player has ever <u>duplicated</u> his trademark "sky-hook."

   C. a person or animal that is markedly unusual or deformed

4. An all-around player, Abdul-Jabbar brought grace, <u>agility</u>, and versatility to the center position.

   D. an awkward and inexperienced youth

5. Although <u>labeled</u> "unsexy" by Abdul-Jabbar himself, the shot became one of the most effective weapons in all of sports.

   E. impressive and often frightening

6. Alcindor was viewed as something of a <u>freak</u> by his schoolmates.

   F. pronounce judgment on

7. After <u>dominating</u> New York high school basketball at Power Memorial, he enrolled at UCLA.

   G. go beyond or exceed

8. He easily won the NBA <u>Rookie</u> of the Year honor.

   H. develop into a distinctive entity; take form

9. He left the game as its all-time scorer, which may never be <u>surpassed</u>.   I. rule or govern

10. The second Abdul-Jabbar dynasty was about to <u>take shape</u>.   J. make or do or perform again

Exercise 2

Select one word or phrase for each blank from a list of choices given below.

| arrival | take shape | overprotective | trade | illiteracy |
| retirement | beliefs | converted | surpassed | freak |

Abdul-Jabbar was one of the greatest basketball players in the world. He was born in 1947 in New York City. He was the only child of an **1.**_____ mother and a strict father. As the tallest kid in the Harlem school system, he was viewed as something of a **2.**_____ by his schoolmates. Later he enrolled at UCLA and simply ruled the college ranks. In the 1969 NBA Draft, he was picked by the Milwaukee Bucks as the first overall choice. With his **3.**_____, the Bucks soon became a strong team in the league. In 1971, he **4.**_____ from Catholicism to Islam.

Despite his success in Milwaukee, Abdul-Jabbar was unhappy due to the lack of people who shared his religious and cultural **5.**_____ and wanted out. He requested a **6.**_____ to either New York or Los Angeles, and was later sent to the Lakers in 1975. The second Abdul-Jabbar dynasty was about to **7.**_____. In Los Angeles, he and his teammates won five NBA championships and thus established the "Lakers dynasty".

Abdul-Jabbar's **8.**_____ marked the end of an era for the NBA. He left the game as its all-time scorer, which may never be **9.**_____. Since retiring, Abdul-Jabbar has authored several books, worked in the entertainment business and served as a "basketball ambassador", working in various capacities such as a coach and broadcaster as well as helped to fight hunger and **10.**_____. In 1995, Abdul-Jabbar was elected to the Naismith Memorial Basketball Hall of Fame.

Exercise 3

Translate the following sentences into English.

1. 他只有努力学习才能保持在同学中的领先地位。(ahead of)
2. 他们给公司带来了创新理念。(bring to)
3. 我父亲把一间卧室改成了书房。(convert to)
4. 没有人取得比他更大的成就。(no... than...)
5. 他的退役标志着NBA 一个时代的结束。(mark)

Text B

NBA All-Star Game

The NBA All-Star Game is a basketball exhibition game hosted every February by the National Basketball Association (NBA), matching the league's star players from the Eastern Conference against their counterparts from the Western Conference. Each conference team consists of 12 players, making it 24 in total. It is the featured event of NBA All-Star Weekend. NBA All-Star Weekend is a three-day event which goes from Friday to Sunday. The All-Star Game was first staged at the Boston Garden on March 2, 1951.

The starting lineup for each squad is selected by a fan ballot, while the reserves are chosen by a vote among the head coaches from each squad's respective conference. Coaches are not allowed to vote for their own players. If a selected player is injured and cannot participate, the NBA commissioner selects a replacement.

The head coach of the team with the best record in each conference is chosen to lead their respective conference in the All-Star Game, with a prohibition against repeated appearances. The coach of the team with the next best record serves instead.

History

The idea of holding an All-Star Game was conceived during a meeting between NBA president Maurice Podoloff, NBA publicity director Haskell Cohen and Boston Celtics owner Walter A. Brown. In order to regain public attention to the league, Cohen suggested the league host an exhibition game featuring the league's best players, similar to Major League Baseball's All-Star Game. The NBA All-Star Game became a success.

Features of the All-Star Game

The Game is played under normal NBA rules, but there are notable differences from an average game. Since the starting All-Stars are selected by fan votes, players sometimes start the game at atypical positions.

The player introductions are usually accompanied by a significant amount of fanfare, including lighting effects, dance music, and pyrotechnics. Special uniforms are designed for the game each year. Gameplay usually involves players attempting spectacular slam dunks and alley oops. Defensive effort is usually limited and the final score of the game is generally much higher than an average NBA game. The fourth quarter of the game is often played in a more competitive fashion, if the game is close.

Halftime is also longer than a typical NBA game due to musical performances by popular

artists. Recent guests have included Justin Bieber, Michael Jackson, Beyoncé, Mariah Carey, Shakira, Rihanna, and Christina Aguilera.

Events of All-Star Weekend

Friday

NBA All-Star Celebrity Game: First held in 2003, the game features retired NBA players, WNBA players, actors, musicians, and athletes from sports other than basketball.

Rising Stars Challenge: The 2012 game debuted a new name, the "Rising Stars Challenge", and a new format.

Saturday

Slam Dunk Contest: This competition showcases the creativity and athletic ability of some of the league's youngest best dunkers.

Three-Point Contest: The league's best three point shooters shoot five basketballs from five different spots around the three-point line.

Skills Challenge: The Skills Challenge pits selected players in a timed obstacle course of dribbling, shooting and passing. Agility, quickness and accuracy all come into play.

Sunday

The NBA All-Star Game: Eastern Conference vs. Western Conference. Up to now, the Eastern Conference leads with a record of 37 wins and 28 losses.

Word Bank

featured	[ˈfiːtʃərd]	adj.	特定的；被作为特色的
lineup	[ˈlaɪn ʌp]	n.	阵容；一组人
squad	[skwɑːd]	n.	小队；五人组（篮球队的非正式说法）；班
ballot	[ˈbælət]	n.	投票；投票总数
commissioner	[kəˈmɪʃənər]	n.	理事；委员；行政长官；总裁
replacement	[rɪˈpleɪsmənt]	n.	代替者；更换
prohibition	[ˌproʊəˈbɪʃn]	n.	禁止；禁令；禁酒
conceive	[kənˈsiːv]	v.	构思；怀孕
publicity	[pʌbˈlɪsəti]	n.	宣传，宣扬；公开；广告
atypical	[ˌeɪˈtɪpɪkl]	adj.	不合规则的；非典型的
fanfare	[ˈfænfer]	n.	喇叭或号角嘹亮的吹奏声；吹牛，炫耀
pyrotechnics	[ˌpaɪrəˈtekniks]	n.	烟火制造术；各种烟火
spectacular	[spekˈtækjələr]	adj.	壮观的，惊人的；公开展示的
debut	[deɪˈbjuː]	v.	初次登台
showcase	[ˈʃoʊkeɪs]	v.	使展现；在玻璃橱窗陈列

| pit | [pɪt] | v. 使竞争；窖藏；使凹下 |
| dribbling | [ˈdrɪbl] | n. 控球；漏泄 |

Phrase

be accompanied by	伴随有，附有，带着；相伴而生
slam dunk	[篮球]跳跃扣篮（亦作 slam-dunk）
alley oop	空中接力（等于 alley-oop）
come into play	开始活动；开始起作用

Proper Names

Eastern Conference	东部赛区
Western Conference	西部赛区
Boston Garden	波士顿花园球场
Major League Baseball's All-Star Game	美国职业棒球大联盟全明星赛
NBA All-Star Celebrity Game	NBA 全明星名人赛
Rising Stars Challenge	新秀挑战赛
Slam Dunk Contest	扣篮大赛
Three-Point Contest	三分大赛
Skills Challenge	技巧挑战赛

Critical Reading and Thinking

Read the text and decide whether the following statements are true (T) or false (F).

1. _____ The NBA All-Star Game is held in February each year.

2. _____ The starting lineup for each squad is selected by the head coaches from each squad's respective conference.

3. _____ If a head coach is chosen to lead a team in the All-Star Game in one year, he can still serve as head coach in the next year.

4. _____ The purpose of holding the NBA All-Star Game is to regain public attention to the league.

5. _____ The NBA All-Star Game is quite different from an ordinary game.

6. _____ Players often wear their usual uniforms in the NBA All-Star game.

7. _____ Players usually attempt to show their special skills and talents in the game such as slam dunks and alley oops.

8. _____ The fourth quarter of the game is often played more casually, if the game is close.

9. _____ The NBA All-Star Weekend lasts three days.

10. _____ The slam dunk shows the creativity and athletic ability of the NBA's best young dunkers.

Translation

Translate the following sentences into Chinese.

1. The NBA All-Star Game is a basketball exhibition game hosted every February by the National Basketball Association (NBA).

2. The starting lineup for each squad is selected by a fan ballot, while the reserves are chosen by a vote among the head coaches from each squad's respective conference.

3. The Game is played under normal NBA rules, but there are notable differences from an average game.

4. The player introductions are usually accompanied by a significant amount of fanfare, including lighting effects, dance music, and pyrotechnics.

5. Defensive effort is usually limited, and the final score of the game is generally much higher than an average NBA game.

Part Three — Listening and Speaking

Task 1

Word Bank

score	[skɔːr]	v. 得分；记分
rebound	[rɪˈbaʊnd]	n. 篮板球
assist	[əˈsɪst]	n. 助攻
marvelous	[ˈmɑːrvələs]	adj. 了不起的，非凡的
retire	[rɪˈtaɪər]	v. 退休，退役
shooter	[ˈʃuːtər]	n. 射手
court	[kɔːrt]	n. 球场；法院

Listen to a conversation between two students talking about a basketball game and answer the following questions.

1. What was the result of the game?
2. How many points did Kobe score?
3. When does Kobe plan to retire?
4. How did the student get the news?
5. What do they think of Kobe?

Task 2

Word Bank

professional	[prəˈfeʃənl]	*adj.* 专业的；职业的，职业性的
league	[liːg]	*n.* 联盟
conference	[ˈkɑːnfərəns]	*n.* 会议；协商，讨论；联盟
vote-getter	[voʊtˈgetər]	*n.* 吸引选票的候选人
Michael Jordan		迈克尔·乔丹（美国篮球明星）
Larry Bird		拉里·伯德（美国篮球明星）
Tim Duncan		蒂姆·邓肯（美国篮球明星）
Kobe Bryant		科比·布莱恩特（美国篮球明星）

Listen to a passage about the National Basketball Association (NBA) and decide whether the following statements are true (T) or false (F).

1. _____ The National Basketball Association (NBA) was founded on June 6, 1949.
2. _____ All the 30 teams are located in the United States.
3. _____ Each team plays 82 games in the regular season.
4. _____ Players who get the most votes are given a starting spot on the All-Star team.
5. _____ The playoffs begin in June every year.

Task 3

Listen to the five sentences from the recording, repeat each sentence after it is spoken, and then write them down.

1. _____.
2. _____.
3. _____.
4. _____.
5. _____.

Notes (I)

Notes are usually short hand-written letters left for our family members, roommates, colleagues, and other people to give them a brief message. They are usually simple and brief, avoiding redundant information; therefore, even though they may share some similarities with letters in the format, the language used in notes is colloquial and informal. Occasions on which notes are necessary include asking for a favor, showing thanks, making an appointment, apologizing, leaving a telephone message, etc.

A possible format is as follows:

```
                                                    Date
Salutation
Body


                                               (closing)
                                               Signature
```

Sample

```
                                                Sept. 20th
Carl,
    I am going to take part in the semi-final of the campus basketball match Saturday
afternoon. Sorry we can't go to the movies at that time. Maybe next time.


                                                       Reed
```

Follow-up Writing

Robin is your basketball teammate. Your team is going to have the semi-final, so you want him to join in the training on Court No. 2 from 4 p.m. to 6 p.m. this afternoon. Leave him a note to inform him of the time and venue.

Part One: Knowledge Preparation

Race walking is a long-distance discipline within the sport of athletics. It is different from running in that one foot must appear to be in contact with the ground at all times. This is assessed by race judges. Race walking is typically held on either roads or on running tracks. Common distances vary from 3,000 meters up to 100 kilometers. There are two race walking distances contested at the Summer Olympics: the 20 kilometers race walk (men and women) and 50 kilometers race walk (men only). Both are held as road events.

The sport emerged from a British culture of long-distance competitive walking known as pedestrianism, which began to develop the rule set that is the basis of the modern discipline around the mid-19th century. Since the mid-20th century onwards, Russian and Chinese athletes have been among the most successful on the global stage, with Europe and parts of Latin America producing most of the remaining top level walkers. To achieve competitive speeds, race walkers must attain cadence rates comparable to those achieved by world-class 800 meters runners.

竞走是一项长距离的田径运动项目，它与跑步的区别在于竞走运动员必须始终保持至少有一只脚与地面接触，竞走裁判会对此进行评判。竞走运动通常在公路或者跑道上进行，距离从3公里至100公里不等。夏季奥运会中，竞走比赛分为20公里（男子竞走和女子竞走）和50公里（仅有男子竞走）两种赛程，都是公路赛。

竞走起源于英国的长距离步行比赛活动。19世纪中期，步行比赛活动的一系列规则逐渐形成，成为如今竞走项目的基础。20世纪中期以来，俄罗斯和中国田径选手在世界舞台上大放异彩，欧洲和部分拉丁美洲选手也不甘示弱。要想具备有竞争力的速度，竞走运动员必须使自己的步伐保持与世界级800米运动员相当的水平。

Unit 3
Race Walking

Part Two — Reading

Text A

Race Walkin

1. Race walking is not just walking fast or speed walking. It is a defined technique. It is also a competition sport where you can win races at the local level and up through the Olympic Games. Race walking provides opportunities to compete and to achieve national standards for people of all ages.

2. There are two rules that govern race walking. The first dictates that one foot must be on the ground at all times. If a judge sees that both feet are off the ground, the walker will get a lifting violation. The second rule requires that the knee must be straight from the time the leading foot touches the ground until it passes vertically under the body. If a judge sees a bent knee, the walker will be disqualified.

3. The IAAF rules spell out the differences between running and walking. Competitors who cross the boundary from walking to running during a race walk are cited for "lifting" infractions. Basically, the walker's front foot must be on the ground when the rear foot is raised. Also, the front leg must straighten when it makes contact with the surface. Race walking judges can caution competitors who push the envelope by showing them a yellow paddle. The same judge cannot give a walker a second caution. Instead, when a walker clearly fails to comply with the walking rules, the judge sends a red card to the chief judge. Three red cards, from three different judges, will result in a competitor's disqualification. Additionally, the chief judge can disqualify an athlete inside the stadium (or in the final 100 meters of a race that takes place solely on a track or on a road course) if the competitor clearly violates the walking rules, even if the competitor has not accumulated any red cards. All judging is done by the eye of the judge and no outside technology is used in making judging decisions. In all other aspects, a race walk follows the same rules as any other road races.

4. Race walking, an exercise with a greatly reduced incidence of injury, provides unparalleled benefits. At high speeds, race walking actually involves a higher rate of muscle activity and burns more calories per mile than does jogging at the same pace. A study shows that race walking burns 120 to 130 calories per mile, more than running which burns between 100 and 110 and certainly

more than freestyle walking. Race walking also works the upper body as well as the lower body, for in order to walk at high speeds, one has to pump his/her arms vigorously. It helps tone and strengthen the muscles in the arms, neck, and chest as it burns calories, but it doesn't pound the knee joints the way running does, for the race walker always has one foot on the ground when race walking.

Word Bank

defined	[dɪˈfaɪnd]	adj. 有定义的，确定的；清晰的
local	[ˈloʊkl]	adj. 当地的；局部的；地方性的
standard	[ˈstændərd]	n. 标准；水准
dictate	[ˈdɪkteɪt]	v. 命令，规定；口述；使听写
violation	[ˌvaɪəˈleɪʃn]	n. 违反；妨碍
vertically	[ˈvɜːrtɪkli]	adv. 垂直地
bent	[bent]	adj. 弯曲的
disqualified	[dɪsˈkwɑːlɪfaɪd]	adj. 不合格的；被取消资格的
boundary	[ˈbaʊndri]	n. 边界；范围；分界线
infraction	[ɪnˈfrækʃn]	n. 违反
rear	[rɪr]	adj. 后方的；后面的
straighten	[ˈstreɪtn]	v. 变直
caution	[ˈkɔːʃn]	v. 警告
stadium	[ˈsteɪdiəm]	n. 体育场；露天大型运动场
solely	[ˈsoʊlli]	adv. 单独地，唯一地
accumulate	[əˈkjuːmjəleɪt]	v. 积攒，积累
unparalleled	[ʌnˈpærəleld]	adj. 无比的，无双的

Phrases

spell out	清楚地解释；详细说明
be cited for	被列为
make contact with	接触；与……联系
push the envelope	触碰界限
yellow paddle	黄牌
comply with	照做，遵守
in all other aspects	在其他方面

Unit 3
Race Walking

Proper Names

IAAF (International Association of Athletics Federations) 国际田径联合会

Task 1 Text Organization

Read the text and fill in the blanks.

Paragraphs	Key Words	Supporting Details
Beginning (Para. 1)	_____ to race walking	It is a _____ as well as a _____.
Body (Paras. 2–3)	_____ of race walking	• One foot must be _____. • The knee must be _____.
End (Para. 4)	_____ of race walking	Race walking involves a higher _____ and burns _____ and it also works _____.

Task 2 Reading Comprehension

Exercise 1

Read the text and decide whether the following statements are true (T) or false (F).

1. _____ Race walking is a competition sport in the Olympic Games.
2. _____ Race walking rules require that a competitor's one foot must be on the ground at all times.
3. _____ The knee can be bent from the time the leading foot touches the ground until it passes vertically under the body.
4. _____ Any three red cards will result in a competitor's disqualification.
5. _____ The judges use their eyes to make an evaluation of the race walkers and report fouls.

Exercise 2

Read the text and answer the following questions.

1. What are the two rules of race walking?
2. In which condition will competitors be cited for "lifting" infractions?
3. In which condition will competitors receive a yellow paddle?
4. In which condition will competitors be disqualified?
5. What are the benefits of race walking?

37

Task 3 Language in Use

Match the underlined words in the left column with their corresponding meanings in the right column.

1. You can win races at the <u>local</u> level and up through the Olympic Games.

2. Race walking also provides opportunities to compete and to achieve national <u>standards</u> for people of all ages.

3. The first <u>dictates</u> that one foot must be on the ground at all times.

4. If a judge see that both feet are off the ground, the walker will get a lifting <u>violation</u>.

5. It passes <u>vertically</u> under the body.

6. Race walking provides <u>unparalleled</u> benefits.

7. If a judge sees a bent knee, the walker is <u>disqualified</u>.

8. One has to <u>pump</u> his/her arms vigorously.

9. It helps <u>tone</u> and strengthen the muscles in the arms.

A. a basis for comparison; a reference point against which other things can be evaluated

B. radically distinctive and without equal

C. an act that breaks or is contrary to (a rule, principle, treaty, etc.)

D. give a healthy elasticity to

E. move up and down, like a handle or a pedal

F. relating to or applicable to or concerned with the administration of a city or town or district rather than a larger area

G. prevent sb. from doing sth., usually because he or she has broken a rule or is not able enough

H. state or order something

I. in a vertical direction

Select one word or phrase for each blank from a list of choices given below.

| boundary | caution | spell out | comply with | infractions |
| accumulated | rear | additionally | straighten | yellow paddle |

    The IAAF rules **1.**_____ the differences between running and walking. Competitors who cross the **2.**_____ from walking to running during a race walk are cited for "lifting" **3.**_____. Basically, the walker's front foot must be on the ground when the

4._____ foot is raised. Also, the front leg must **5.**_____ when it makes contact with the surface. Race walking judges can **6.**_____ competitors who push the envelope by showing them a **7.**_____. The same judge cannot give a walker a second caution. Instead, when a walker clearly fails to **8.**_____ the walking rules, the judge sends a red card to the chief judge. Three red cards, from three different judges, will result in a competitor's disqualification. **9.**_____, the chief judge can disqualify an athlete inside the stadium (or in the final 100 meters of a race that takes place solely on a track or on a road course) if the competitor clearly violates the walking rules, even if the competitor has not **10.**_____ any red cards.

Exercise 3

Translate the following sentences into English.

1. 竞走并不是简单地快速行走，它是一项包含明确技巧的运动。(defined technique)
2. 衡量竞走有两条规则。(govern)
3. 最重要的是，当竞走者的后脚抬起时，前脚不得离地。(rear foot)
4. 在其他方面，竞走规则和其他公路赛规则相同。(road race)
5. 裁判不能借助任何外界技术设备帮助判断，只能依靠自己的眼睛来判断运动员是否犯规。(outside technology)

Race Walking vs. Power Walking

Race walking is often confused with power walking, as the two activities are basically similar. The difference lies in the fact that power walking is practiced principally to produce a training effect, whilst race walking is a competitive discipline within the sport of athletics. Nevertheless, both of them are excellent exercises because they burn far more calories than regular walking and they cause far fewer injuries than running. Race walking and power walking each require different techniques than regular walking. Race walking's techniques are formal rules because race walking is a competitive sport, while power walking is not.

Power Walking Techniques

Regular walking is a natural activity and the walking speed is limited for approximately 4.5 mph. Power walkers, though, can reach 5.5 mph by consciously changing their posture, taking faster steps, and swinging their arms. If you want to try power walk, you should walk so upright that your head is level and only your eyes move when you look at your feet. Taking 135 to 150

steps per minute will improve your speed more than longer strides, which can strain your buttocks, hamstrings and lower back. Swinging your arms while they are bent 90 degrees and keeping your elbows in a fixed position will also improve your speed.

Race Walking Techniques

While race walking, the head should remain level and relaxed, with eyes looking approximately 20 yards in front of the body. Swing arms loosely and vigorously, pivoting from the shoulders. As for the torso, you should keep the body posture relaxed and straight, avoiding leaning too far forward or sitting back, which can result in a loss of power. The proper way to achieve a faster pace is to increase leg speed, not over-striding, which means to maintain the natural stride length for your body and increase the number of strides per minute. Gradually, work towards achieving 160 steps per minute. Over time, you may reach 180–200 steps per minute. Landing too far forward of the torso is over-striding and an inefficient technique that will slow the pace, cause "soft knee", and possibly lead to an injury of the iliopsoas and popliteal (behind the knee) muscles.

Improving Your Speed

Race walking requires more arm strength and leg strength than power walking. Consequently, race walkers need to do more strength exercises. The best strength exercises for race walkers and power walkers include chest presses and bicep curls for your upper body, squats for your lower body, and abdominal crunches for both. Experts recommend strength exercises 20 minutes daily four times weekly, but prospective competitive athletes should do more. The American College of Sports Medicine recommends 8 to 12 repetitions of 8 to 10 different strength exercises two to three times weekly to improve your performance in all aerobic activities, including walking.

Word Bank

principally	['prɪnsəpli]	adv. 主要地；大部分
discipline	['dɪsəplɪn]	n. 训练；学科；项目；纪律
approximately	[ə'prɑːksɪmətli]	adv. 大约，近似地，近于
consciously	['kɑːnʃəsli]	adv. 自觉地；有意识地
posture	['pɑːstʃər]	n. 姿势；态度；情形
swing	[swɪŋ]	v. 摇摆，摆动
stride	[straɪd]	n. 大步；步幅
strain	[streɪn]	v. 拉紧；竭力
buttock	['bʌtək]	n. 臀部
hamstring	['hæmstrɪŋ]	n. 肌腱；蹄筋
elbow	['elboʊ]	n. 肘

vigorously	['vɪɡərəsli]	*adv.* 精力旺盛地；活泼地
pivot	['pɪvət]	*v.* 在枢轴上转动；随……转移
torso	['tɔːrsoʊ]	*n.* 躯干
lean	[liːn]	*v.* 倚靠
iliopsoas	[ɪlɪoʊ'soʊrs]	*n.* [解剖] 髂腰肌
popliteal	[pɒp'lɪtɪrl]	*adj.* 膝后窝的
squat	[skwɑːt]	*v.* 蹲，蹲下
prospective	[prə'spektɪv]	*adj.* 未来的；预期的
aerobic	[e'roʊbɪk]	*adj.* 需氧的；有氧健身的

Phrases

be confused with	与……混淆
lie in	在于
bicep curls	二头肌训练
abdominal crunches	仰卧起坐

Critical Reading and Thinking

Read the text and decide whether the following statements are true (T) or false (F).

1. _____ Race walking and power walking are the same.
2. _____ Power walking burns far more calories than running.
3. _____ Race walking and power walking each require different techniques.
4. _____ Regular walkers can reach 5.5 mph by consciously changing their posture.
5. _____ Taking faster steps per minute will strain your buttocks, hamstrings and lower back.
6. _____ During race walking, leaning too far forward or sitting back can result in a loss of power.
7. _____ Over-striding is an efficient technique to improve the speed, but may cause "soft knee", and possibly lead to an injury of the iliopsoas and popliteal muscles.
8. _____ Race walkers need to do more strength exercises.
9. _____ Chest presses, bicep curls, squats, and abdominal crunches are the best strength exercises.
10. _____ The American College of Sports Medicine recommends strength exercises 20 minutes daily four times weekly.

Translation

Translate the following sentences into Chinese.

1. The difference lies in the fact that power walking is practiced principally to produce a training effect, whilst race walking is a competitive discipline within the sport of athletics.

2. Power walkers, though, can reach 5.5 mph by consciously changing their posture, taking faster steps, and swinging their arms.

3. Taking 135 to 150 steps per minute will improve your speed more than longer strides, which can strain your buttocks, hamstrings and lower back.

4. The proper way to achieve a faster pace is to increase leg speed, not over-striding, which means to maintain the natural stride length for your body and increase the number of strides per minute.

5. Landing too far forward of the torso is over-striding and an inefficient technique that will slow the pace, cause "soft knee", and possibly lead to an injury of the iliopsoas and popliteal (behind the knee) muscles.

Part Three Listening and Speaking

Task 1

Word Bank

marathon	[ˈmærəθɑːn]	n. 马拉松赛跑；耐力的考验
apparently	[əˈpærəntli]	adv. 显然地
toe	[toʊ]	n. 脚趾；足尖
sign up for		注册，选课；报名参加

Listen to a conversation between two students talking about race walking and answer the following questions.

1. What event is going to be held in the city next week?
2. Who can participate in the event?
3. How is race walking different from running?
4. What are the rules in race walking?
5. What problem does the student have when he starts learning race walking?

Unit 3
Race Walking

Task 2

Word Bank

emphasize	['emfəsaɪz]	v. 强调，着重
competitive	[kəm'petətɪv]	adj. 竞争的；比赛的
workout	['wɜːrkaʊt]	n. 锻炼；练习
jogging	['dʒɑːgɪŋ]	n. 慢跑
participation	[pɑːrˌtɪsɪ'peɪʃn]	n. 参与
incredibly	[ɪn'kredəbli]	adv. 难以置信地；非常地
motion	['moʊʃn]	n. 运动，移动

Listen to a passage about race walking and complete the sentences with the information you hear.

1. Race walking is an event of the sport of _____.
2. There are two race walking distances at the _____: the 20 kilometers race walk and 50 kilometers race walk.
3. Race walking can be a good exercise for everyone because it doesn't require _____; and it will give you a much better _____ than regular walking.
4. Studies have shown that race walking causes _____ than running.
5. Apart from low injury risks, race walking has many other _____, such as controlling weight, _____, saving workout time and so on.

Task 3

Listen to the five sentences from the recording, repeat each sentence after it is spoken, and then write them down.

1. _____.
2. _____.
3. _____.
4. _____.
5. _____.

Notes (II)

Notes are usually informal, but there are also occasions when formal notes are required. Notes asking for leave are one of the examples. Like other notes, notes asking for leave may include date, salutation, body as well as closing and signature. But in notes asking for leave, the body part not only puts forward the request of asking for leave, but also offers the reason or reasons. The language should not be too casual since such notes are usually submitted to people superior to you, but should be considered relatively formal.

Here is an example asking for sick leave:

Sample

March 16, 2009

Dear Mr. White,

    I am Lewis from Sports Education Class. I would like to apply for a three-day sick leave as I am down with a bad flu. I have enclosed the doctor's certificate and I promise to catch up with other classmates in all the courses.

    Thank you!

Yours,
Lewis

Follow-up Writing

David sprained his ankle this morning and can't attend Prof. Wang's class in the afternoon. Write a note asking for sick leave in his name.

Unit 4
Recreational Sports

Part One — Knowledge Preparation

Recreational sports are those activities of which the primary purpose is participation, with the related goals of improving physical fitness, and enhancing social involvement. Recreational sports are usually perceived as being less stressful, both physically and mentally, on the participants. There are lower expectations regarding both performance and commitment to the sport in the recreational sphere. In theory, there is a clear demarcation between purely recreational pursuits and competitive sports, where emphasis will be centered on the achievement of success and the attainment of physical skills through rigorous training. Competitive sport involves not only contests, but also advances as a central tenet that the athlete or team will continually seek progress and advancement to a higher level. A recreational sport is more popular in the world today due to its accessibility and variety. Golf, bowling, rock climbing, sports dancing, and skateboarding are all part of recreational sports.

休闲体育是重在参与的体育活动，旨在强身健体、社交娱乐，这些目的通常比活动本身更重要。人们大多认为对于参与者来说，休闲体育在精神和身体上压力较小。在娱乐氛围下，对于成绩和投入程度的要求也相对较低。理论上说，竞技体育和休闲体育界限分明。竞技体育重在比赛成绩和通过艰苦训练获得的体育技能。竞技体育不仅仅只是比赛而已，它更进一步的核心信条在于运动员或运动团队将会一直向着更高目标做出努力。如今休闲体育因其平易近人且内容多样而更受欢迎。高尔夫、保龄球、攀岩、体育舞蹈和滑板都属于休闲体育项目。

Part Two — Reading

Sport Climbing

❶ Rock climbing is an activity in which participants climb up, down or across natural rock formations or artificial rock walls. The goal is to reach the summit of a formation or the endpoint of a usually pre-defined route without falling. Due to the length, extended endurance is required and because accidents are more likely to happen on descent than ascent, rock climbers do not usually climb back down the route. It is very rare for a climber to down climb, especially on the larger multiple pitches. Professional rock climbing competitions have the objectives of either completing the route in the quickest possible time or attaining the farthest point on an increasingly difficult route. By comparing to some other climbing sports, rock climbing is generally differentiated by its sustained use of hands to support the climber's weight as well as to provide balance.

2 Sport climbing is a form of rock climbing that relies on permanent anchors fixed to the rock for protection. This is in contrast to traditional climbing where climbers must place removable protection as they climb. Sport climbing emphasizes strength, endurance, gymnastic ability and technique over adventure, risk and self-sufficiency. For the majority of sport climbers, sport climbing offers an easier, more convenient experience which requires less equipment, less in the way of technical skills and lower levels of mental stress than traditional climbing.

Sport Climbing vs. Traditional Climbing

3 Less gear required: Because the emphasis is on the moves, sport climbers don't place their own protection, but clip into preplaced bolts with metal hangers. This allows the lead climber to progress upward without the worry and hassle of carrying a full rack of gear and placing protection like one would with traditional climbing.

4 Accessibility: Sport routes can be found indoors or out, on nearby, accessible rock crags or on artificial walls at a gym or a competition arena. Climbers can enjoy being on the "sharp end" of the rope—that is, leading the climb—without knowing how to place chocks or cramming devices.

5 Falling: In sport climbing, it's normal and expected that you'll fall, often repeatedly, as you work out a difficult move. In traditional climbing, you would typically take care not to fall and stress the anchors you are placing.

6 The first sport climbing competitions were organized in the former USSR in the late 1940s. These events were focused on Speed Climbing, and were mostly dedicated to Soviet climbers until the 1980s, and in 1989 the first ever Climbing World Cup was held.

7 Today's sport climbing competitions are held in three different disciplines: Bouldering, where athletes conquer the greatest number of obstacles without rope; Lead, where athletes seek to climb highest on the wall; and finally Speed, where the fastest climber is declared the winner. The relatively young sport has not only added to the popularity of climbing walls everywhere, it has greatly improved rock climbing standards too.

8 The International Federation of Sport Climbing (IFSC) is the international governing body for the sport of competitive climbing. It was founded in Frankfurt on January 27, 2007 by 48 member federations, and is a continuation of the International Council for Competition Climbing, which had been in existence from 1997 to 2007 and was a part of the Union Internationale des Associations d'Alpinisme (UIAA). The major competitions organized by the IFSC are the World Championship,

World Cup, European Championship, World Youth Championship, and European Youth Cup.

9. On August 3, 2016, sport climbing was added to the 2020 Summer Olympics program.

Word Bank

formation	[fɔːrˈmeɪʃn]	n. 构造；[地] 地层；形成；队形
artificial	[ˌɑːrtɪˈfɪʃl]	adj. 人造的；虚伪的；武断的
summit	[ˈsʌmɪt]	n. 顶点；最高阶层
endpoint	[ˈendˌpɔɪnt]	n. 端点
endurance	[ɪnˈdʊrəns]	n. 忍耐，忍耐力；耐性
descent	[dɪˈsent]	n. 下降；下坡；家世；血统；衰落；继承
ascent	[əˈsent]	n. 上升；上坡路；晋升，提升
objective	[əbˈdʒektɪv]	adj. 客观的；真实的
		n. 目标；目的
attain	[əˈteɪn]	v. 实现；获得；达到
sustain	[səˈsteɪn]	v. 支持；承受，经受；维持；认可
anchor	[ˈæŋkər]	n. 锚；依靠；新闻节目主播
		v. 抛锚；停泊；用锚系住；担任（广播电视新闻节目）的主持人
clip	[klɪp]	v. 夹住；剪短；疾驰；猛击
		n. 夹子；回形针；钳；修剪；（羊毛的）剪下量
bolt	[boʊlt]	n. 门闩；螺栓
		v.（突然）逃离；闩住；狼吞虎咽
		adv. 挺直地
hassle	[ˈhæsl]	n. 困难；争吵；麻烦
		v. 烦扰；麻烦
gear	[gɪr]	n. 传动装置；齿轮；排挡；工具，装备
		v. 调整，使适应于；以齿轮连起
accessibility	[əkˌsesəˈbɪləti]	n. 可以得到；易接近
crag	[kræg]	n. 峭壁，危岩
arena	[əˈriːnə]	n. 竞技场
chock	[ˌtʃɑːk]	n. 楔子，木楔，楔形木垫
		v. 用楔子垫阻
		adv. 紧紧地
camming	[ˈkæmɪŋ]	n. 凸轮系统
transition	[trænˈzɪʃn]	n. 转变；过渡
bouldering	[ˈboʊldərɪŋ]	n. 抱石攀岩运动
conquer	[ˈkɑːŋkər]	v. 征服，克服；战胜，得胜
obstacle	[ˈɑːbstəkl]	n. 障碍；绊脚石

Unit 4
Recreational Sports

Phrases

be differentiated by	差别在于（按……来区分）
rely on	依靠；信赖
in contrast to	和……对比，与……相反
be committed to	献身于；忠于某一立场
be in existence	存在；现有的；目前世界上的

Proper Names

USSR (Union of Soviet Socialist Republics)	苏联
IFSC (International Federation of Sport Climbing)	国际攀岩联合会
World Championship	世界锦标赛
World Cup	世界杯
European Championship	欧洲锦标赛
European Youth Cup	欧洲青年杯

Task 1 Text Organization

Read the text and fill in the blanks.

Paragraphs	Key Words	Supporting Details
Beginning (Paras. 1–2)	Two concepts: Rock climbing _____ climbing	• Rock climbing is _____. (1) The goal is _____. (2) The objective of rock climbing competition is to _____. • _____ is a form of rock climbing that relies on permanent anchors fixed to the rock for protection. (1) It emphasizes _____. (2) The benefit is _____.

49

Body (Paras. 3–5)	Differences between sport climbing and traditional climbing	• _____. • _____. • _____. • Sport climbing attracts more people to join into this climbing activity.
End (Paras. 6–9)	Sport climbing competition	• History of sport climbing competition: The first climbing World Cup was held in _____. • The three disciplines of sport climbing competitions are _____, _____, and _____. • The international governing body of sport climbing competition is _____. It organizes _____. • On _____, sport climbing was added to _____.

Task 2 Reading Comprehension

Exercise 1

Read the text and decide whether the following statements are true (T) or false (F).

1. _____ Rock climbing is an old-fashioned adventure; it is a form of sport climbing.
2. _____ The goal of sport climbing is to reach the summit of a formation or the endpoint of a usually pre-defined route without falling.
3. _____ It's normal to fall in sport climbing especially when you work out a difficult move.
4. _____ Accidents are more likely to happen on the descent than the ascent route.
5. _____ In rock climbing, permanent anchors are fixed to the rock for protection.

Exercise 2

Read the text and answer the following questions.

1. What are the differences between traditional rock climbing and sport climbing?
2. What are the responsibilities of a lead climber in traditional climbing?
3. Where was the first sport climbing competition held?
4. What are the three disciplines of today's sport climbing competitions?
5. What is the international governing body of sport climbing competitions?

Unit 4
Recreational Sports

Task 3 Language in Use

Exercise 1

Match the underlined words in the left column with their corresponding meanings in the right column.

1. The goal is to reach the <u>summit</u> of a formation or the endpoint of a usually pre-defined route without falling.

2. Due to the length, extended <u>endurance</u> is required.

3. Rock climbing is generally differentiated by its <u>sustained</u> use of hands to support the climber's weight as well as to provide balance.

4. Sport climbing is a form of rock climbing that relies on permanent <u>anchors</u> fixed to the rock for protection.

5. With increased <u>accessibility</u> to climbing walls and gyms more climbers now enter the sport through indoor climbing than outdoor climbing

6. Sport routes can be found indoors or out, on nearby, accessible rock <u>crags</u> or on artificial walls at a gym or a competition arena.

7. In bouldering, athletes <u>conquer</u> the greatest number of obstacles without rope to declare a winner.

8. All of us at the IFSC are deeply <u>committed</u> to meeting the challenges ahead.

9. Professional Rock climbing competitions have the objectives of either completing the route in the quickest possible time or <u>attaining</u> the farthest point on an increasingly difficult route.

A. the ability to keep doing something difficult, unpleasant, or painful for a long time

B. cause or allow something to continue for a period of time

C. take control or possession of foreign land

D. the quality or characteristic of something that makes it possible to approach, enter, or use it

E. device or method for attaching a climber, a rope, or a load to the climbing surface

F. the highest point of a mountain

G. a high, rough mass of rock that sticks out from the land around it

H. reach or succeed in getting something

I. loyal and willing to give time and energy to something that one believes in

Exercise 2

Select one word for each blank from a list of choices given below.

| sufficient | anchors | contrast | formations | artificial |
| endurance | relies on | transition | accessibility | summit |

Rock climbing is an activity in which participants climb up, down or across natural rock 1._____ or 2._____ rock walls. The goal is to reach the 3._____ of a formation or the endpoint of a usually pre-defined route without falling. Due to the length, extended 4._____ is required. Sport climbing is a form of rock climbing that 5._____ permanent 6._____ fixed to the rock for protection. In 7._____ to traditional climbing, it requires less gear, expects repeated falling in a difficult move and is more accessible. With increased 8._____ to climbing walls and gyms, more climbers now enter the sport through indoor climbing than outdoor climbing and the 9._____ from indoor to sport climbing is much easier than that to traditional climbing, because the techniques and equipment used for indoor leading are nearly 10._____ to sport climb.

Exercise 3

Translate the following sentences into English.

1. 和去年相比，今年参加运动攀岩比赛的人数大大增加了。(in contrast to)
2. 分开后，他们特别依赖电话联系。(rely on)
3. 随着高等教育在国内的普及，越来越多的人进入了大学。(with increased accessibility to)
4. 年轻人的加入使运动攀岩竞技越来越受欢迎。(added to the popularity of)
5. 他们长得一模一样，但是可以通过运动能力来区分。(is differentiated by)

The World's Craziest Crazy Golf Course?

Paul Gittings

It's crazy golf on an insane scale—a putting green swimming in a giant bowl of noodles and chopsticks, the Great Wall of China for a hazard, a fairway threading through Mayan ruins and a panda-themed hole.

"Traditionalists will probably hate it," says design guru Brian Curley, principal partner in Schmidt-Curley, the company behind the 22 courses that make up the Mission Hills complex in

Hainan Island. "But this is real golf, with real clubs on real fairways," he told CNN.

Fantasy Golf

Curley and his team wanted to come up with something that he felt would appeal to the wider Chinese public and other visitors to the resort. So instead of bunkers, rough and trees, the players will be faced with a replica of the Great Wall of China winding its way the length of a 400-meter par four hole.

That tricky 17th sees the best in the world attempt to hit their ball onto a tiny green surrounded by water, and spectators delight in seeing the likes of Tiger Woods find the lake.

At Mission Hills' new course, set to open in 2014, the water is replaced by an 80-meter wide noodle bowl with 50-meter giant chopsticks. Standing on the tee, players will not know whether to laugh or cry, and the degree of difficulty may not end there.

Wind Machine

Curley is promising the addition of "man made" gale force winds on each tee, adjustable depending on the standards of the players and available by hitting a red button. There is a par-5 threading its way through Mayan ruins, while another green is created in the image of the "Birds Nest" Olympic Stadium. Another hole is styled after China's favorite animal, the panda bear.

On a conventional golf course, the degree of difficulty is often dictated by which tee the player chooses to play from. Leading professionals play from the tees furthest from the hole, while higher handicappers can opt to hit their first shot from much closer.

Curley and his team needed the permission of the owners of the complex before committing to the costly project, but Mission Hills' chairman Dr. Ken Chu is an enthusiastic backer.

"This will be a fun alternative for families, novices and children on holiday," he was quoted in the Asian edition of *Golf Course Industry International*.

Only time will tell if Chu's faith in the project proves founded, but the Mission Hills group has already established itself as a host venue of leading professional tournaments.

Last year the Hainan Island development staged the World Cup teams event for the first time, taking over from the Mission Hills complex at Shenzhen.

This year Shenzhen was the venue of the prestigious HSBC-World Golf Championship event, won by Englishman Ian Poulter.

The Ryder Cup hero conquered the conventional Olazabal course in 21 under par, he will probably be itching to test his mettle on Curley's new wacky creation at the first opportunity.

Word Bank

scale	[skeɪl]	n. 规模；刻度；等级
hazard	['hæzərd]	n. 危险；冒险；危害
fairway	['ferweɪ]	n.（高尔夫球）球道；航路；开阔的通道
traditionalist	[trə'dɪʃənəlɪst]	n. 传统主义者；因循守旧者
guru	['ɡuruː]	n. 古鲁（指印度教等宗教的宗师或领袖）；领袖；专家
bunker	['bʌŋkər]	n. [高尔夫] 沙坑；[军事] 掩蔽壕；煤仓
rough	[rʌf]	n. 深草区；高低不平的路面
replica	['replɪkə]	n. 复制品
par	[pɑr]	n. 标准杆；标准；票面价值；平均数量
		adj. 标准的；票面的
spectator	['spekteɪtər]	n. 观众；旁观者
tee	[tiː]	n. [高尔夫球] 发球的球座；球梯
		v. 将（高尔夫球）置于球座
gale	[ɡeɪl]	n. 狂风；一阵（喧闹，笑声等）
conventional	[kən'venʃənl]	adj. 传统的；惯例的；常规的
handicapper	['hændɪˌkæpə]	n. 裁判人员；（赛马等时）决定优劣条件之人
wacky	['wækɪ]	adj. 乖僻的，古怪的

Phrases

putting green	高尔夫球场果岭
appeal to	吸引；呼吁，恳求；申诉
High-handicapper	高差点球员

Proper Name

Mission Hills complex	观澜湖高尔夫大会

Critical Reading and Thinking

Read the text and decide whether the following statements are true (T) or false (F).

1. _____ The world craziest golf course is built by Schmidt-Curley Company.

2. _____ The new whacky design of the golf course is favored by the traditionalists.

3. _____ Brian Curley is the owner of Schmidt-Curley, the company behind the 22 courses that make up the Mission Hills complex in Hainan Island.

4. _____ Curley and his team wanted to amaze the wider Chinese public and other visitors to the resort by their design.

5. _____ The golf course will be set by the Great Wall.

6. _____ The panda-themed hole is hidden in the Great Wall.

7. _____ Dr. Ken Chu supports Curly and his team to work on this new project.

8. _____ Chu's faith in the project proves to be founded.

9. _____ Hainan Island development staged the World Cup teams event for the first time, taking over from the Mission Hills complex at Shenzhen.

10. _____ Ian Poulter won the champion in the crazy golf course.

Translation

Translate the following sentences into Chinese.

1. Curley and his team wanted to come up with something that he felt would appeal to the wider Chinese public and other visitors to the resort.

2. That tricky 17th sees the best in the world attempt to hit their ball onto a tiny green surrounded by water, and spectators delight in seeing the likes of Tiger Woods find the lake.

3. Curley and his team needed the permission of the owners of the complex before committing to the costly project, but Mission Hills' chairman Dr. Ken Chu is an enthusiastic backer.

4. Only time will tell if Chu's faith in the project proves founded, but the Mission Hills group has already established itself as a host venue of leading professional tournaments.

5. The Ryder Cup hero conquered the conventional Olazabal course in 21 under par, he will probably be itching to test his mettle on Curley's new wacky creation at the first opportunity.

Part Three — Listening and Speaking

Task 1

Word Bank

specialized	['speʃəlaɪzd]	*adj.* 专业的；专门的
ensure	[ɪn'ʃʊr]	*v.* 保证，确保
belay	['biːleɪ]	*v.* 把（登山者）用绳索固定
experienced	[ɪk'spɪriənst]	*adj.* 有经验的

| rent | [rent] | v. 出租，租用 |
| fire away | | 开始讲；开始问 |

Listen to a conversation between two students talking about rock climbing and answer the following questions.

1. What does a climber have to use to ensure safety?
2. What's belaying?
3. What do the new climbers of Ted's club have to learn?
4. How tall are the walls in the rock climbing gym of Ted's university?
5. Where can climbers rent the climbing equipment?

Task 2

Word Bank

demanding	[dɪ'mændɪŋ]	adj. 苛求的，要求高的；吃力的
involve	[ɪn'vɑːlv]	v. 包含；牵涉
strength	[streŋθ]	n. 力量，力气
documentary	[ˌdɑːkju'mentri]	n. 纪录片
wedge	[wedʒ]	n. 楔子；楔形物
nut	[nʌt]	n. 螺母，螺帽；坚果
crack	[kræk]	n. 裂缝
solo	['soʊloʊ]	adj. 独奏的，独唱的；单独的
buildering	['bɪldərɪŋ]	n. 徒手攀爬高楼墙壁（攀岩运动的一种）
boulder	['boʊldər]	n. 大圆石；巨砾

Listen to a passage about the types of rock climbing and complete the sentences with the information you hear.

1. Rock climbing is a physically and mentally demanding sport which involves strength, _____, endurance and _____.
2. In traditional rock climbing, climbers place wedges or nuts into _____.
3. Sport climbing is _____ than traditional climbing.
4. Free solo climbing is like sport climbing without the use of any _____. So, if a climber falls, he or she is likely to be _____.
5. In bouldering and buildering, climbers climb on boulders or the sides of buildings instead of on natural cliffs or _____.

Task 3

Listen to the five sentences from the recording, repeat each sentence after it is spoken, and then write them down.

1. _____.
2. _____.
3. _____.
4. _____.
5. _____.

Part Four Writing

Notices

A notice is usually a written or printed announcement to give information about what is going to happen (e.g. a meeting, a contest, a match, a party, etc.) to the public. Generally speaking, a notice should include three parts: time, location and event, but some details may also be necessary. For tours, information about preparation can be very important; for lectures, background knowledge about the speaker or the topic is very helpful; for schedule changes, the reason should be provided. Notices may take various forms; therefore, they may look quite different.

Sample 1   A notice of a lecture

Essential Skills to Be a Rock Climber

Speaker: John Long

Founding member of "Stonemasters", an elite rock climbing group

Author of *How to Rock Climb!*

Date: Friday, 17th Sept.

Time: 19:00

Venue: Lecture Hall 1, Physical Education Department

All welcome!

Sample 2　A notice of a tour

Rock Climbing Trip

10th April, 2012

　　A rock climbing trip has been arranged to the Golden Rooster Valley in Chengdu from 30th April to 4th May. Club members who are interested in this trip can register by sending e-mails to the following address: rockclimbingclub@sina.com before 15th April. We will accept the first 15 members who have successfully registered via e-mail and send them the detailed arrangement before 20th April.

The Rock Climbing Club

Follow-up Writing

The lecture "Sport Climbing and Rock Climbing" was arranged to be given in Lecture Room #3 at 9:00 a.m. on 9th Oct. But the speaker Prof. Smith Harrison cannot give the lecture because he is required to take part in an international conference on that day. Write a notice to announce the change of the schedule.

Unit 5
Chinese Traditional Sports

Part One: Knowledge Preparation

Chinese martial arts, referred to officially as the Chinese term Wu Shu or popularly as Kung Fu or Wu Gong, are a number of fighting styles that have developed over centuries in China. Wu Shu consists of two separate Chinese characters. Wu means "martial or military", and Shu means "technique, discipline, method or art". Similarly, the term Kung Fu, translated as "effort" and "skill", is also a term to describe combat skill.

The fighting styles are often identified, according to common features, as "families", "sects" or "schools" of martial arts. Examples of such features include physical exercises involving animal mimicry, or training methods inspired by Chinese philosophies, religions and legends.

Chinese martial arts are divided into two main categories. One category which focuses on "chi" manipulation is viewed as internal, while the other category which concentrates on improving muscle and fitness is considered as external. Internal styles include Xingyiquan, Baguazhang, and Taijiquan, which have a close connection to Taoism and the Wudang monastery. In contrast, external styles are closely related to Buddhism and the Shaolin monastery.

中国武术是指在中国发展了几个世纪的一些武打风格，官方称武术，俗称功夫或武功。武术由两个汉字构成，"武"指"尚武的或军事的"，"术"指"技、规、法、艺"。同样，功夫被译为英文的 effort（努力）和 skill（技能），也是用来形容搏斗技能的术语。

根据共性特征，武打风格通常可分为武术的"家""派"或"门"。这些共性特征包括：模仿动物进行的体能训练，或受中国哲学、宗教和传说启发的训练方式。

中国武术主要分为两大类。一类为内家拳，注重"气"的控制；另一类为外家拳，注重肌肉训练，保持体型。内家拳包括形意拳、八卦掌和太极拳，与道教和武当道观联系紧密。而外家拳则与佛教和少林寺密切相关。

Part Two — Reading

Bruce Lee and His Martial Arts

Alex Ben Block

1. When a lifelike figure of Bruce Lee was unveiled at Madame Tussaud's Wax Museum in Hollywood in 2010, his only surviving child, Shannon Lee, noted that her father died shortly before the 1974 premiere of *Enter the Dragon*, the movie that made him the first Asian actor to become a global superstar.

2. Thirty-seven years after his sudden death, Lee's dream has been fulfilled not only in Hollywood but all over the world.

3. He has become an iconic figure alongside Marilyn Monroe and James Dean, whose images are instantly recognizable generations after their death.

4. What is interesting about Bruce Lee is that he is not only remembered for many movies and TV shows in which he starred but also for breaking racial barriers, helping erase stereotypes and his contributions in such areas as mixed martial arts, fitness, health and a philosophy that recognized the commonality of all humanity.

5. The next wave brought Jackie Chan and Jet Li and others who offered their own variation on Lee's legacy but still never quite replaced him as a martial artist or a movie icon.

6. But that was only part of Lee's legacy. His impact was greater than movies. As the first Asian international action star, he smashed the Western stereotype of the Chinese coolie, and provided reason for a whole generation of young Asians, as well as other minorities, to be proud of their heritage.

7. Until Lee, martial arts were a rigid system of schools and styles that fiercely competed to be called the best. Lee created his own style, Jeet Kune Do, which not only took the best of what the Chinese, Japanese, Korean and other martial arts offered but added in elements of boxing, wrestling and even weight lifting. His approach included health foods, running, aerobics and even electrical stimulation of muscles—all of which are common today but were radical in the 1970s. Today it is even taught at the university level in China.

8 His movies stimulated the worldwide growth of martial arts of all kinds, but it went beyond that. It was clear that Lee strived for the invention of mixed martial arts, which flourishes today in multiple forms, such as the Ultimate Fighting Championships.

9 Interestingly, the acceptance of Lee as a hero was not instant in the People's Republic of China. At the time Lee died on July 20, 1973, China was only beginning to open up to the West and Lee was seen as a symbol of decadent Western influence. As China has become more involved with the rest of the world, the Chinese have seen the value of using Lee as a symbol.

10 That was most obvious in 2008 when CCTV ran a 50-part series on the life of Lee. It became the highest rated series in the history of the channel.

11 So the legend of Bruce Lee truly is going to continue through movies, TV shows, musical plays, books, licensed merchandise, martial arts, physical culture and much more.

Word Bank

unveil	[ˌʌnˈveɪl]	v. 揭开；揭幕
premiere	[prɪˈmɪr]	n. 首映式；首映
recognizable	[ˈrekəgnaɪzəbl]	adj. 可辨认的；可认出的
racial	[ˈreɪʃl]	adj. 种族的；人种的
stereotype	[ˈsteriətaɪp]	n. 成见；刻板印象
variation	[ˌveriˈeɪʃn]	n. 变异，变种
legacy	[ˈlegəsi]	n. 遗产
smash	[smæʃ]	v. 粉碎；使破产
coolie	[ˈkuːli]	n.（印度的）苦力；小工
minority	[maɪˈnɔːrəti]	n. 少数民族；少数派
heritage	[ˈherɪtɪdʒ]	n. 遗产；传统
approach	[əˈproʊtʃ]	n. 方法，途径
aerobics	[eˈroʊbɪks]	n. 有氧运动法；健美操
stimulation	[ˌstɪmjuˈleɪʃn]	n. 刺激；激励，鼓舞
flourish	[ˈflɜːrɪʃ]	v. 兴旺；活跃
multiple	[ˈmʌltɪpl]	adj. 多样的；许多的
decadent	[ˈdekədənt]	adj. 颓废的

Unit 5
Chinese Traditional Sports

Phrases

martial arts	武术
weight lifting	举重
strive for	争取，奋斗
become/be involved with	涉及；与……有关
highest rated (TV) series	最高收视率电视连续剧

Proper Names

Bruce Lee	李小龙(1940-1973)，世界武道变革先驱者、武术技击家、武术哲学家、UFC（Ultimate Fighting Championships）开创者、MMA（Mixed Martial Arts）之父、武术宗师、功夫片的开创者和截拳道创始人、华人武打电影演员、中国功夫首位全球推广者、好莱坞首位华人演员。
Madame Tussaud's wax museum	杜莎夫人蜡像馆，位于美国加利福尼亚州洛杉矶好莱坞的中心，成立于1965年，是企业家斯普尼·塞恩（Spoony Singh）提出建造的，是美国唯一的好莱坞明星蜡像馆，蜡像馆内有好莱坞180多个电影明星的蜡像，包括查理·卓别林、迈克尔·杰克逊以及中国明星成龙等。
Hollywood	好莱坞，位于美国西海岸加利福尼亚州洛杉矶郊外，依山傍水，景色宜人。它是世界闻名的电影中心，每年在此举办的奥斯卡颁奖典礼是世界电影的盛会。
Shannon Lee	李香凝，李小龙之女，1969年4月19日生于美国加利福尼亚州洛杉矶市，演员。李小龙去世时，她只有4岁，对于父亲的印象都是后来从照片和电影以及妈妈琳达·埃莫瑞、哥哥李国豪的回忆中得到的。
Enter the Dragon	《龙争虎斗》，1973年嘉禾影业和华纳影业联合制作的一部动作电影，由克洛斯执导，李小龙、石坚、约翰·萨克松等主演。
Jackie Chan	成龙，1954年生于香港中西区，男演员、导演、动作指导、制作人、编剧、歌手。
Jet Li	李连杰，1963年生于中国北京市，演员、武术家、慈善家、商人。
Jeet Kune Do	截拳道，武术明星李小龙生前创立的一类现代武术体系，融合了世界各国拳术，以咏春拳、拳击与击剑作

		为技术骨干，以中国道家思想为主创立的实战格斗体系构想，也是一种全新的思想体系。"截拳道"的意思就是截击对手来拳之道。近代流行的搏击比赛运动及综合格斗更是尊崇李小龙为第一先驱者。
Ultimate Fighting Championships		终极格斗冠军赛（美国本土的一个综合格斗组织，李小龙是公认的 UFC 鼻祖）

Task 1 Text Organization

Read the text and fill in the blanks.

Paragraphs	Key Words	Supporting Details
Beginning (Paras. 1–2)	becoming a global superstar and fulfilling his dream	• the movie that made him the _____ to become a global superstar; • Lee's dream fulfilled not only in Hollywood but _____.
Body (Paras. 3–8)	making great _____	• a _____ alongside Monroe and James Dean; • breaking racial barriers, helping _____ and his contributions in such areas as _____, fitness, health and a philosophy that recognized the commonality of _____; • being not replaced by other _____ or movie icons like Jackie Chan and Jet Li, etc.; • smashing the Western _____ and providing reason for young Asians to be proud of their _____; • creating his own style, _____, which make the best of the advantages of other martial arts or sports; • inventing _____, which flourishes today in multiple forms, such as _____.
End (Paras. 9–11)	greatly impacting the world	• a symbol of _____; • the _____ on the life of Lee becoming the highest rated series in the history of CCTV; • _____ of Bruce Lee through different approaches.

Unit 5
Chinese Traditional Sports

Task 2 Reading Comprehension

Exercise 1

Read the text and decide whether the following statements are true (T) or false (F).

1. _____ The figure of Bruce Lee was revealed at Madame Tussaud's Wax Museum in Hollywood in 2010.
2. _____ Jackie Chan and Jet Li are supposed to replace Bruce Lee as martial artists or movie icons.
3. _____ Lee played a large role in the invention of mixed martial arts, such as the Ultimate Fighting Championships.
4. _____ Bruce Lee was considered as a symbol of heroism in China and Western countries immediately after his death.
5. _____ CCTV ran a 50-part series on the life of Lee, and it became the most popular series in the history of the channel.

Exercise 2

Read the text and answer the following questions.

1. Which movie made Bruce Lee the first Asian actor to become a global superstar?
2. What is the relationship between Bruce Lee and Shannon Lee?
3. When did Bruce Lee's dream come true?
4. Why do people remember Bruce Lee?
5. What did Bruce Lee create as his own style of martial arts?

Task 3 Language in Use

Exercise 1

Match the underlined words or phrases in the left column with their corresponding meanings in the right column.

1. Shannon Lee noted that her father died shortly before the 1974 <u>premiere</u> of "Enter the Dragon", which made him the first Asian actor to become a global superstar.

   A. an offensive name for an unskilled Asian laborer

2. He has become an <u>iconic</u> figure alongside Marilyn Monroe and James Dean.

   B. the first public performance of a new play or movie

3. He is not only remembered for many movies and TV shows in which he starred but also for breaking <u>racial</u> barriers.

4. Many people offered their own <u>variation</u> on Lee's legacy but still never quite replaced him as a martial artist or a movie icon.

5. He smashed the Western stereotype of the Chinese <u>coolie</u>.

6. Until Lee, martial arts were a rigid system of schools and styles that <u>fiercely</u> competed to be called the best.

7. His approach included health foods, running, <u>aerobics</u> and even electrical stimulation of muscles.

8. It was clear that Lee strived for the invention of mixed martial arts, which <u>flourishes</u> today in multiple forms.

9. At the time Lee died on July 20, 1973, China was only beginning to open up to the West and Lee was seen as a symbol of <u>decadent</u> Western influence.

10. As China has become more <u>involved with</u> the rest of the world, the Chinese have seen the value of using Lee as a symbol.

C. in a way marked by extreme and violent energy

D. exercise that increases the need for oxygen

E. be connected with in some way

F. important or impressive because it seems to be a symbol of something

G. marked by excessive self-indulgence and moral decay

H. the same thing presented in a slightly different form

I. grow stronger

J. of or related to genetically distinguished groups of people

Exercise 2

Select one word for each blank from a list of choices given below.

| recognizable | martial | variation | legacy | minorities |
| barriers | iconic | stereotypes | commonality | smashed |

He has become an **1.**_____ figure alongside Marilyn Monroe and James Dean, whose images are instantly **2.**_____ generations after their death.

What is interesting about Bruce Lee is that he is not only remembered for many movies and TV shows in which he starred but also for breaking racial **3.**_____, helping erase **4.**_____ and his contributions in such areas as mixed **5.**_____ arts, fitness, health and a philosophy that recognized the **6.**_____ of all humanity.

The next wave brought Jackie Chan and Jet Li and others who offered their own **7.**_____ on Lee's legacy but still never quite replaced him as a martial artist or a movie icon.

But that was only part of Lee's **8.**_____. His impact was greater than movies. As the first Asian international action star he **9.**_____ the Western stereotype of the Chinese coolie, and provided reason for a whole generation of young Asians, as well as other **10.**_____, to be proud of their heritage.

Exercise 3

Translate the following sentences into English.

1. 迪士尼电影公司于本周二在香港为该片举行了全球首映仪式。(premiere)
2. 他成了和雷锋一样的偶像人物，全心全意为人民服务。(iconic)
3. 一个大公司应该始终以争取精益求精的品质和完善的售后服务为宗旨。(strive for)
4. 目前，应帮助小学生对环境采取积极的应对措施。(approach)
5. 他通过多种声音和风格成功地在上海举办了一次音乐会。(multiple)

Magic Taijiquan

As a famous national intangible cultural heritage, Taijiquan is an application of the Chinese Taoist philosophy of Yin Yang in the human body. According to this philosophy, everything is made up of two opposites, but entirely complementary, elements of yin and yang, such as light and dark, fire and water. They work in a relationship in perpetual balance. Taijiquan uses this concept to form a motion meditation for one's mind and body.

The Chen Style of Taijiquan is the oldest form of all the well-recognized family styles, which include the Yang, Wu, Sun and Wu-Hao. Chen Style Taijiquan is characterized by its silk reeling, alternating speed motion and bursts of power. It is the only style of Taijiquan practiced mainly for combat, followed by health. The rest of the styles are practiced more for the purpose of health.

The practice of Taijiquan combines flowing movements and breathing techniques with the guidance of mental and spiritual awareness to bring about a workout that benefits the mind, body, and soul. Primarily a martial art, Taijiquan is very effective for self-defense, but it is also a powerful weapon against disease in helping one maintain health and balance internal energy. Daily training makes the muscles and bones become softer and more pliable, and it especially causes the

breath to become natural. These are the results of disciplining and refining the essence, energy and spirit to the end of one's days.

    For many practitioners, the combat aspects of Taijiquan are of considerable interest. For others the focus is not chiefly on a martial art, but on a meditative exercise for the body. In Chinese philosophy and medicine there is a concept of "chi", a vital force that animates the body. One of the avowed aims of Taijiquan is to foster the circulation of this "chi" within the body. It is believed that by doing so one's health and vitality are enhanced. This "chi" circulates in patterns that are closely related to the nervous and vascular system, and thus closely connected with the practice of acupuncture and other oriental healing arts. Another aim of Taijiquan is to foster a calm and tranquil mind, through the focus on its precise execution. Learning to do it correctly provides a practical avenue for learning about balance, alignment, fine-scale motor control, rhythm of movement, and the genesis of movement from the body's vital center, etc. Thus the practice of Taijiquan can also contribute to being able to better stand, walk, move and run, etc. in other spheres of life.

    As one of the best known internal martial arts, Taijiquan can be practiced quickly for martial applications or slowly for reducing mental stress and maintaining physical health. Obviously, the popularity of Taijiquan will take another quantum leap as more people experience its enjoyment and benefits.

Word Bank

complementary	[ˌkɑmplɪˈmentri]	adj. 补足的，补充的
perpetual	[pərˈpetʃuəl]	adj. 永久的；永恒的
meditation	[ˌmedɪˈteɪʃn]	n. 冥想；沉思
combat	[ˈkɑːmbæt]	n. 战斗；争论
pliable	[ˈplaɪəbl]	adj. 柔韧的；柔软的
refine	[rɪˈfaɪn]	v. 精炼，改善
practitioner	[prækˈtɪʃənər]	n. 从业者
philosophy	[fəˈlɑsəfi]	n. 哲学；哲理
animate	[ˈænɪmeɪt]	v. 使有生气；使活泼
avowed	[əˈvaʊd]	adj. 公开宣布的；公开承认的
vitality	[vaɪˈtæləti]	n. 活力；生命力
enhance	[ɪnˈhæns]	v. 提高；加强
vascular	[ˈvæskjələr]	adj. [生物] 血管的
acupuncture	[ˈækjupʌŋktʃər]	n. 针刺；[中医] 针刺疗法
oriental	[ˌɔːriˈentl]	adj. 东方的；东方人的
tranquil	[ˈtræŋkwɪl]	adj. 平静的；安宁的

avenue	[ˈævənuː]	n.（比喻达到某物的）途径，手段
alignment	[əˈlaɪnmənt]	n. 校准
genesis	[ˈdʒenəsɪs]	n. 发生；起源
sphere	[sfɪr]	n. 范围

Phrases

silk reeling	缠丝劲
bursts of power	发劲
vital force	生机，生命力
healing art	医术
quantum leap	巨大突破

Proper Names

Taijiquan (Taiji Quan; Tai Chi)	太极拳，中国武术中的一种拳法，属于国家级非物质文化遗产。它以中国传统儒、道哲学中的太极、阴阳辩证理念为核心思想，集颐养性情、强身健体、技击对抗等多种功能为一体，结合易学的阴阳五行之变化，中医经络学，古代的导引术和吐纳术形成的一种内外兼修、柔和、缓慢、轻灵、刚柔相济的中国传统拳术。
Chen Style Taijiquan	陈氏太极拳，一种起源于明末的汉族拳术。
essence, energy and spirit	哲学与医学上是指"精""气""神"，也是道教内丹学术语。"精""气""神"三者之间是相互滋生、相互助长的。从中医学讲，人的生命起源是"精"，维持生命的动力是"气"，而生命的体现就是"神"的活动。所以说精充气就足，气足神就旺；精亏气就虚，气虚神也就少。
chi	东方医学、武术等中的"气"是指人生命运动的根本和动力，它不是一个独立的概念，而是有形的气与无形的意相结合的混合体，是身体各个部位密切的配合，是经过长期科学的训练而形成的肢体神经信息迅速的传导，是肌肉纤维组织在意念的引导下力量的定向传输。

Critical Reading and Thinking

Read the text and decide whether the following statements are true (T) or false (F).

1. _____ Taijiquan is an application of the Taoist philosophy of Yin Yang, which is used to form a motion meditation for the mind and body.

2. _____ The Yang Style is the only style of Taijiquan practiced mainly for combat, followed by health. The rest of the styles are practiced more for health reasons.

3. _____ Primarily a martial art, Taijiquan is very effective for fighting with others, but it is also a powerful weapon against disease and to maintain health.

4. _____ Many Taijiquan practitioners concentrate on doing a meditative exercise for the body.

5. _____ In Chinese philosophy and medicine, there exists the concept of "chi", a vital force that makes the body lively or more cheerful.

6. _____ People believe that Taijiquan can help them improve their health and energy by inventing "chi" within the body.

7. _____ The only purpose of doing Taijiquan is to develop a calm and peaceful mind by focusing on its precise execution.

8. _____ The practice of Taijiquan can help to bring about better standing, walking, moving and running.

9. _____ Taijiquan is one of the most famous martial arts of the external systems in China.

10. _____ Taijiquan will become more popular because more people find it pleasant and advantageous.

Translation

Translate the following sentences into Chinese.

1. As famous national intangible cultural heritage, Taijiquan is the application of the Chinese Taoist philosophy of Yin Yang in the human body.

2. Chen Style Taijiquan is characterized by its silk reeling, alternating speed motion and bursts of power.

3. Daily training makes the muscles and bones become softer and more pliable, and it especially causes the breath to become natural.

4. For others the focus is not chiefly on a martial art, but on a meditative exercise for the body.

5. The popularity of Taijiquan will take another quantum leap as more people experience its enjoyment and benefits.

Part Three: Listening and Speaking

Task 1

Word Bank

cultivate	['kʌltɪveɪt]	v. 培养；陶冶
originate	[ə'rɪdʒɪneɪt]	v. 发源；发生
fascinating	['fæsɪneɪtɪŋ]	adj. 迷人的；吸引人的
name after		以……命名
trace back to		追溯到；追溯到……的起源

Listen to a conversation between two students talking about Tai Chi and answer the following questions.

1. How long has Li Ming been practicing Tai Chi?
2. Where does Li Ming come from?
3. What is Tai Chi?
4. What are the benefits of practicing Tai Chi?
5. How many major styles of Tai Chi are there in China?

Task 2

Word Bank

opponent	[ə'poʊnənt]	n. 对手；反对者
engage	[ɪn'ɡeɪdʒ]	v. 从事
civilization	[ˌsɪvələ'zeɪʃn]	n. 文明；文化
dynasty	['daɪnəsti]	n. 朝代
innovator	['ɪnəveɪtər]	n. 创新者
fencing	['fensɪŋ]	n. 剑术
instructor	[ɪn'strʌktər]	n. 指导员；教练
edema	[ɪ'diːmə]	n. 水肿
painkiller	['peɪnkɪlər]	n. 止痛药
Mars	[mɑːrz]	n. 战神
Roman	['roʊmən]	n. 罗马人；古罗马语

savate	[sə'væt]	法式踢打术
derive from		源出，来自
Yellow Emperor		黄帝
Wing Chun		咏春拳

Listen to a passage about martial arts and choose the best answer to each question.

1. What's the general purpose of designing martial arts?

   A. Starting wars.

   B. Training for combat.

   C. Defeating opponents and defending against threats.

   D. Engaging in fighting, war, and hunting.

2. Which country do people often associate martial arts with?

   A. Asia.   B. China.

   C. India.   D. Japan.

3. Which one of the following statements about Bruce Lee is NOT true?

   A. He had great ability to act in popular movies and the television series.

   B. He was an innovator in the martial arts.

   C. He was the founder of Jeet Kune Do.

   D. He refused to teach Chinese martial arts to Westerners.

4. What caused the death of Bruce lee?

   A. A brain edema.   B. A bad injury.

   C. An accident.   D. A fight.

Task 3

Listen to the five sentences from the recording, repeat each sentence after it is spoken, and then write them down.

1. _____.
2. _____.
3. _____.
4. _____.
5. _____.

Part Four — Writing

Posters (I)

A poster is a large picture, notice, or advertisement attached to a wall to be displayed in a public place. There are posters for political, commercial, entertaining and educational purposes. Being informative or persuasive, successful posters are always eye-catching and impressive. For successful posters, both textual and graphic elements should be considered, although a poster may be either completely graphical or wholly text. Information presented verbally in posters may be in words, phrases or clauses as long as they are accurate and clear. Sentences can also be used, but usually not complex or complicated in structure.

Sample 1   A poster of a notice

Football Match

Thursday, May 25

A friendly football match will be held between our faculty team and the team of Chemical Engineering College on our football field at 5:00 p. m. on Saturday, May 27, 2006.

All are warmly welcome!

Students' Union of
School of Life Science

Sample 2 A poster of an activity

LOCAL REC LEAGUE

PRESENTS

THE 10TH ANNUAL

BOWLING

Invitational

SATURDAY, OCTOBER 8TH @ 10:00 AM

OPEN TO EVERYONE

THE LOCAL BOWLING ALLEY - 61 MAIN ST

RULES AND REGULATIONS:

* players per team

* 2 women players minimum per team

* Minimum age is 12

* Lanes are limited. Preregistration is not required but recommended.

For more information:

LIEM CRAVENS can be reached on his call or at the Local Bowling Alley

www.thelocalbowlingalley.com/invitational

Follow-up Writing

Write a text for a poster based on the information given below without considering the design of the pattern.

There will be an annual holiday Christmas Dance named "Rockin' Around the Christmas Tree" held at St. Allen's College's gymnasium (Maple Street, Seattle, WA) on Saturday, 11th December from 7 p.m. to 12 p.m. There is no need to worry about the traffic since taxis are always available. The organizer will offer food and refreshments. There will also be prizes for participants who take the tickets with them. Tickets are sold at the Front Office. Tickets bought in advance cost $10 per person and $25 for a couple. Those bought at door cost $12 per person and $30 for a couple.

Unit 6
Sports Culture

Part One — Knowledge Preparation

The origins of the Olympic Games date back to at least the eighth century BC. Dedicated to the Greek god Zeus, they took place on the plains of Olympia in the Peloponnese every four years. Sports included running, wrestling, boxing, and a primitive form of martial art known as pancratium, equestrian competitions, and pentathlon.

The ancient Olympic Games fell into decline when Rome conquered Greece in 146 BC and were finally abolished in 393 AD by Emperor Theodosius I. The site of the Games, Olympia, sank into oblivion, and was ravaged by earthquakes and floods. It wasn't until 1,500 years later that the modern Olympic Games were born in Athens in 1896, featuring 311 participants from 13 nations. The Games slowly grew under the guidance of Pierre de Coubertin, who founded the International Olympic Committee in 1894.

In the 1900 Games, women were allowed to take part in for the first time. By 1924, the Olympic Games in Paris had captured the public's attention. More than 3,000 athletes from 43 nations took part in the Games. It wasn't until Rome 1960 that the Olympics were broadcast live across Europe, and Tokyo 1964 that they reached a worldwide audience.

Today, the Games are the world's largest sporting celebration, with more than 10,500 athletes from 206 countries taking part in Rio 2016.

奥运会的起源可以回溯到至少公元前8世纪时。为纪念希腊天神宙斯，奥运会每四年在伯罗奔尼撒半岛的奥林匹亚平原上举行一次。运动项目包括赛跑、摔跤、拳击、角斗（一种古老的武术形式）、马术竞赛以及五项全能。

公元前146年，罗马攻占希腊，古代奥运会开始没落，最终于公元393年被狄奥多西一世大帝废除。奥运会举办地奥林匹亚被人们所遗忘，被地震和洪水摧毁。直到1500年后，现代奥运会于1896年在雅典诞生，来自13个国家的311位参赛者见证了这一盛会。奥运会在顾拜旦的领导下逐渐成长，于1894年成立了国际奥林匹克委员会。

在1900年奥运会上，女性首度被允许参赛。1924年，巴黎奥运会吸引了大众的目光，来自43个国家的超过3000名运动员参加了这一体育盛会。直到1960年的罗马奥运会，奥运赛事开始在全欧洲直播。到1964年东京奥运会时，奥运会才在全球直播。

如今，奥运会已是全球最大的体育盛事，2016年里约奥运会吸引了来自206个国家的10 500多名运动员参加。

Unit 6
Sports Culture

Part Two — Reading

Olympic Gold Medals or Olympic Spirit?

① To trace the origins of the modern Olympic Games we must travel back nearly 3,000 years in time to ancient Greece, when young men proved their physical powers and fighting skills by competing in sporting activities. But the ancient Olympic Games were not solely about sporting endeavor; they were also used as an opportunity for the Greeks to honor their gods, particularly Zeus, the king of the Greek gods, whose massive statue stood in the valley of Olympia.

② Many of the sports practiced by the ancient Greeks still exist in an adapted form today, including wrestling, boxing, running, jumping and throwing contests. But there are important differences. Modern-day spectators would be astonished if the athletes competed naked like the ancient Greeks did.

③ Although the Olympic Games fell into decline after Greece was conquered by the Roman Empire in 146 BC, the spirit of the Games did not die away altogether. Interest in the Games was revived in the 19th century after a wealthy Greek philanthropist paid for the renovation of an ancient stadium in Athens. The result was the 1859 Olympic Games staged between just two countries: Greece and the Ottoman Empire. International interest grew, and in 1894 a French aristocrat called Pierre de Coubertin hosted a congress at the Sorbonne University in Paris in order to suggest a new modern Olympic Games. De Coubertin's ideas were met with international approval and the first Olympic Games of the modern age took place in Athens in 1896.

④ Since then, the Olympics have gone from strength to strength, with competitors from all over the world taking part in, and billions more watching on television. Every four years, people come together for two weeks of competition, and fight for national pride in the Olympic Games. Athletes from around the world have the chance to gain national and international fame while capturing the attention of spectators around the world.

⑤ Everybody loves a winner. Across the world, countries are greeting their Olympic gold medalists with joy and acclaim after the 2016 Rio Olympic Games. In Singapore, Joseph Schooling, the city-state's first ever gold medalist, has become a national hero and is greeted with a standing ovation in Parliament.

6 Yet amid all this celebration of triumph and victory, it is important to remember the words of Pierre de Coubertin, the founder of the modern Olympics, who said, "The most important thing in the Olympic Games is not winning, but taking part."

7 In the heats of the women's 5000 m in the 2016 Rio Olympics, when Abbey D'Agostino of the U.S. and Nikki Hamblin of New Zealand tripped and fell—the two athletes helped each other to get up and finish the race. They have received more worldwide attention for their outstanding display of the Olympic spirit than they would have done for winning medals.

8 The truth is that any athlete who has made it to the Olympics—let alone an Olympic final—has achieved something remarkable. Enormous dedication and effort are needed to obtain qualification of the Olympic Games. And it is even harder to accept defeat with good grace. Those athletes who remain true to the spirit of de Coubertin, despite all these pressures, are just as inspirational as the winners of gold medals.

Word Bank

trace	[treɪs]	v. 追溯，追踪
origin	[ˈɔːrɪdʒɪn]	n. 起源，开端
endeavor	[ɪnˈdevər]	n. 尽力，竭力
massive	[ˈmæsɪv]	adj. 大量的；巨大的，厚重的；魁伟的
astonish	[əˈstɑːnɪʃ]	v. 惊讶
decline	[dɪˈklaɪn]	n. 下降；衰退
revive	[rɪˈvaɪv]	v. 复兴；复活
renovation	[ˌrenəˈveɪʃn]	n. 革新
aristocrat	[əˈrɪstəkræt]	n. 贵族
fame	[feɪm]	n. 名声，名望
capture	[ˈkæptʃə]	v. 捕捉；获得
medalist	[ˈmedəlɪst]	n. 奖牌获得者
acclaim	[əˈkleɪm]	n. 欢呼，喝彩；称赞
ovation	[oʊˈveɪʃn]	n. 热烈欢迎；大喝彩
triumph	[ˈtraɪʌmf]	n. 胜利，凯旋
remarkable	[rɪˈmɑːrkəbl]	adj. 卓越的；非凡的
dedication	[ˌdedɪˈkeɪʃn]	n. 奉献；献身

Phrases

die away	减弱，消失
meet with	符合；偶然遇见
from strength to strength	越来越强大；不断取得成功

Unit 6
Sports Culture

Proper Names

Olympia	奥林匹亚（希腊一地名）
Zeus	宙斯（希腊神话中的主神）
Baron Pierre de Coubertin	皮埃尔·德·顾拜旦（法国著名教育家、国际体育活动家、教育学家和历史学家、现代奥林匹克运动的发起人）

Task 1 Text Organization

Read the text and fill in the blanks.

Paragraphs	Key Words	Supporting Details
Beginning (Paras. 1–2)	The _____ of the Olympic Games	• origin: (1) The Olympic Games date back to _____. (2) Ancient Olympic Games were not only _____, but also _____. (3) ancient Greek sports v.s. modern Many of the sports practiced by the ancient Greeks still _____.
Body (Paras. 3–4)	The _____ of the Olympic Games	• process: (1) Although the Olympic Games fell into decline in 146 BC, the spirit of the games _____. (2) Interest in the games was _____ _____. (3) In 1894 a French aristocrat called Pierre de Coubertin _____ and the first Olympic Games _____.
(Paras. 5–7)	What is the _____ ____ of the Olympic Games?	• Examples of Olympic competitors who lost gold medals won _____ because of _____.
End (Para. 8)	The _____ of the Olympic spirit	Those athletes who _____ are just _____ the winners of gold medals.

Task 2 Reading Comprehension

Exercise 1

Read the text and decide whether the following statements are true (T) or false (F).

1. _____ In ancient Greece, the Olympic Games were used as a way for the Greek to honor their gods.
2. _____ Many of the ancient Greek sports still exist in an adapted form in modern Olympic Games.
3. _____ As the Olympic Games fell into decline after Greece was conquered by the Roman Empire in 146 BC, the spirit of the Games disappeared as well.
4. _____ International interests in the Olympic Games grew because a French aristocrat called Pierre de Coubertin hosted a congress at the Sorbonne University in Paris in order to suggest a new modern Olympic Games.
5. _____ Only gold medalists win worldwide respect in the Olympic Games.

Exercise 2

Read the text and answer the following questions.

1. What did ancient Greek young men do to prove their physical power?
2. Were ancient Olympic Games only used for doing sports competition?
3. Do any ancient Greek sports still exist today?
4. Why is Joseph Schooling considered as a national hero in Singapore?
5. What is the spirit of Pierre de Coubertin?

Task 3 Language in Use

Exercise 1

Match the underlined words in the left column with their corresponding meanings in the right column.

1. But the ancient Olympic Games were not solely about sporting <u>endeavor</u>.
   A. imparting a divine influence on the mind and soul

2. Modern-day spectators would be <u>astonished</u> if the athletes competed naked like the ancient Greeks did.
   B. someone who watches something, especially a sports event

Unit 6
Sports Culture

3. Interest in the Games was <u>revived</u> in the 19th century after a wealthy Greek philanthropist paid for the renovation of an ancient stadium in Athens.

4. Every four years, the world comes together for two weeks of competition, and fight for national <u>pride</u> in the Olympic Games.

5. Athletes from around the world have the chance to gain national and international fame while capturing the attention of <u>spectators</u> around the world.

6. Across the world, countries are greeting their Olympic gold medalists with <u>joy</u> and acclaim after the 2016 Rio Olympic Games.

7. Yet amid all this celebration of <u>triumph</u> and victory, it is important to remember the words of Pierre de Coubertin.

8. Athletes from around the world have the chance to gain national and international <u>fame</u> while capturing the attention of spectators around the world.

9. Those athletes who remain true to the spirit of de Coubertin, despite all these pressures, are just as <u>inspirational</u> as the winners of gold medals.

10. Enormous <u>dedication</u> and effort are needed to obtain qualification of the Olympic Games.

C. the state or quality of being widely honored and acclaimed

D. amaze; shock

E. an attempt to do something, especially something new or original

F. (economy, a business, a trend, or a feeling) becomes active, popular, or successful again

G. the act of binding yourself (intellectually or emotionally) to a course of action

H. a feeling of satisfaction that you have because you or people close to you have done something good or possess something good

I. something or someone that makes you feel happy or gives you great pleasure

J. a great success or achievement, often one that has been gained with a lot of skill or effort

 Exercise 2

Select one word for each blank from a list of choices given below.

| interruption | physical | power | moral | honor |
| happened | accomplish | informal | definitely | profit |

The first modern Olympic Games was held in Athens in 1896 and only thirteen nations participated. Besides the host nation, participants were tourists who **1.**_____ to

be in Greece at the time. Though the whole affair was 2._____ and the standard was not high, the old principle of amateur sport was kept up. Since then the games had been held every four years except during the 3._____ of the two World Wars. This was 4._____ a departure from the old Olympic spirit when wars had to stop and made way for the Games. The Games have grown enormously in scale and 5._____ performances have now reached unprecedented heights. Unfortunately the same cannot be said about their 6._____ standard. Instead of Olympia, the modern Games are now held in different cities all over the world. Inevitably politics and commercialism get involved as countries vie each other for the 7._____ to hold the Games because of the political prestige and commercial 8._____ out of them. In the 11th Games held in Berlin in 1936, Hitler who had newly come to 9._____ in Germany tried to use the occasion for his Nazi propaganda. For the first time the Olympic flame was brought all the way from Olympia to the Games site in relays, a marathon journey now often taking months to 10._____.

 Exercise 3

Translate the following sentences into English.

1. 为了追溯现代奥林匹克运动会的起源，我们必须回到 3000 年以前的古希腊。(trace back)
2. 这部影片为他赢得了国际声誉。(fame)
3. 我们获得与当地音乐家见面的机会，并聆听了他们的演奏。(meet with)
4. 我们有很大的潜力，可以再接再厉。(from strength to strength)
5. 世界各国正愉快地以欢呼声迎接他们的奥运冠军。(acclaim)

Text B

China's Traditional Sports Culture

China's traditional sports have a variety of activities and a long history with their own system. They develop, descend and go on with their own cultural styles and are one of the outstanding representatives of sports cultures.

Chinese traditional sports have developed on the basis of natural economy, patriarchal-clan-system-and-origin society, the national spirits and Chinese philosophy. They mainly consist of Wushu, Daoyin or Qigong, folk games and the traditional sports of ethnic minorities.

Chinese traditional sports culture is an important component of the world sports culture. It

records the developmental process of human society in these aspects: from skills in Wushu to Daoyin that regulates breath, from the native games in the form of exercises that mainly meet the need of entertainment to the traditional sports of minorities that are "living fossils".

Many official competitions in modern Olympic Games such as soccer, running, weightlifting, swimming, wrestling, fencing, archery, and skating, etc. can be found in Chinese traditional sports, and some of them have a much longer history in China than in the Western countries. Every sport has its ample and specific cultural connotations.

However, the vigor of traditional sports in China is languishing in real life. Certain folk sports have emerged and perished and the imperial sports are disappearing because of the fads that they lack theoretical instructions and sports systems. Another reason is that these traditional sports are not competed in the Olympic Games, so they are being ignored and abandoned, and their development is slowing down.

But, Chinese traditional sports are always attracting the world with their special spirit and charm. It is believed that Chinese traditional sports can drag themselves out of the sea of doubt, go out into the world and would be gradually accepted by people all over the world.

Word Bank

nationalist	['næʃnəlɪst]	*adj.* 民族主义的；国家主义的
regulate	['regjuleɪt]	*v.* 调节；规定
fossil	['fɔsəl]	*n.* 化石；僵化的事物；顽固不化的人
		adj. 化石的；陈腐的，守旧的
archery	['ɑːtʃəri]	*n.* 箭术，射箭
ample	['æmp(ə)l]	*adj.* 丰富的；足够的；宽敞的
connotation	[ˌkɑːnə'teɪʃn]	*n.* 内涵；隐含意义
vigor	['vɪgər]	*n.* [生物] 活力，精力
languish	['læŋgwɪʃ]	*v.* 凋萎；失去活力
perish	['perɪʃ]	*v.* 死亡；毁灭
imperial	[ɪm'pɪriəl]	*adj.* 帝国的；皇帝的
fad	[fæd]	*n.* 时尚；一时的爱好；一时流行的狂热
theoretical	[ˌθiːə'retɪkl]	*adj.* 理论的
abandon	[ə'bændən]	*v.* 放弃；放任
drag	[dræg]	*v.* 拖累；拖拉

Phrases

patriarchal clan system	宗法制度
on the basis of	根据；基于……

ethnic minority	少数民族
in the form of	以……的形式
out of doubt	毫无疑问
slow down	减速，放慢速度

Proper Names

Wushu	武术
Daoyin	中医导引术
Qigong	气功

Critical Reading and Thinking

Read the text and decide whether the following statements are true (T) or false (F).

1. _____ China's traditional sports have a long history with their own cultural styles.

2. _____ Traditional sports in China have developed on the basis of natural philosophy.

3. _____ Traditional sports in China include folk games and traditional sports of ethnic minorities.

4. _____ China's traditional sports play an important role in the world sports culture.

5. _____ China's traditional sports are merely exercises for the need of entertainment.

6. _____ Many official competitions in modern Olympic Games can be found in Chinese traditional sports.

7. _____ Some traditional Chinese sports are disappearing because of the lack of theoretical instructions and perfect sports systems.

8. _____ Chinese traditional sports will have a bright future and attract more people from all over the world.

Translation

Translate the following sentences into Chinese.

1. China's traditional sports have a variety of activities and a long history with their own system.

2. Chinese traditional sports culture is an important component of the world sports culture.

3. Each traditional sport in China has its ample and specific cultural connotations.

4. China's traditional sports are always attracting the world with their special spirit and charm.

Part Three — Listening and Speaking

Task 1

Word Bank

ancient	[ˈeɪnʃənt]	adj. 古代的；古老的
propose	[prəˈpoʊz]	v. 求婚；提议；计划
participant	[pɑːrˈtɪsɪpənt]	n. 参与者
incredible	[ɪnˈkredəbl]	adj. 极好的；难以置信的
International Olympic Committee		国际奥林匹克委员会

Listen to a conversation between two students talking about the origin of the Olympic Games and answer the following questions.

1. When was the first ancient Olympic Games held?
2. When and where were the first modern Olympic Games held?
3. Who is considered the father of the modern Olympics?
4. How many people participated in the first modern Games?
5. When were women first allowed to compete at the Olympics?

Task 2

Word Bank

invade	[ɪnˈveɪd]	v. 侵略；侵袭
boycott	[ˈbɔɪkɑːt]	v. 联合抵制；拒绝参加
protester	[prəˈtestər]	n. 抗议者；反对者
criticize	[ˈkrɪtɪsaɪz]	v. 批评；评论
homosexual	[ˌhoʊməˈsekʃuəl]	n. 同性恋者 adj. 同性恋的
delegation	[ˌdelɪˈgeɪʃn]	n. 代表团
Sochi	[ˈsotʃi, ˈsɔtʃɪ]	索契（俄罗斯黑海东岸港市）
Vancouver	[vænˈkuːvər]	温哥华（加拿大城市）
Soviet	[ˈsoʊviet]	adj. 苏维埃的；苏联的
Afghanistan	[æfˈgænɪstɑːn]	阿富汗（亚洲国家）

| Billie Jean King | 比利·简·金（美国女子网球运动员） |

Listen to a VOA news report about the 2014 Winter Olympics in Sochi, and choose the best answer to each question.

1. When did the 2014 Winter Olympic Games open?

   A. On Sunday night.   B. On Saturday night.

   C. On Monday night.   D. On Friday night.

2. Which one of the following statements about Sochi is NOT true?

   A. It is a city on the Black Sea.

   B. It is a popular area for vacation travelers.

   C. It is extremely cold in the winter.

   D. It can be warm and hot in the summer.

3. How much does the 2014 Winter Games cost?

   A. At least fifty billion dollars.

   B. At least fifteen billion dollars.

   C. Seven billion dollars.

   D. Seventeen billion dollars.

4. When was the last time the Olympic Games were held in Russia?

   A. In 1918.   B. In 1980.

   C. In 1988.   D. In 1992.

5. What was criticized by protesters as the Games began?

   A. President Barack Obama.

   B. Discussion of homosexuality.

   C. Russia's treatment of homosexuals.

   D. Billie Jean King.

Task 3

Listen to the five sentences from the recording, repeat each sentence after it is spoken, and then write them down.

1. _____.
2. _____.
3. _____.
4. _____.
5. _____.

Posters (II)

As mentioned in Unit 5, language and pictures are two essential elements for conceiving an attractive poster. Impressive posters are elaborate works of arts, combining text and graphs most of the time. Although the posters illustrated in Unit 5 offer clear and accurate information about relevant activities, they are not eye-catching due to the lack of pictures and colors. Therefore, special attention should also be paid to the form of a poster. Now, appreciate the following two samples, and compare Sample 2 with that in Unit 5, and the samples will present the differences.

Sample 1 A handmade poster

Sample 2　A printed poster

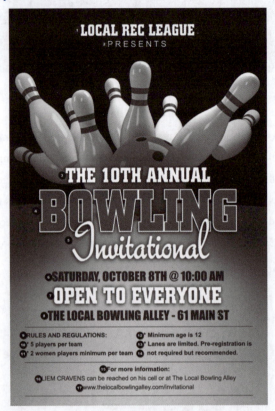

Put what you have produced in Unit 5 down on a piece of paper with your own design.

Unit 7
Sports Science

Part One Knowledge Preparation

Sports science (also sport science) is a discipline that studies how the healthy human body works during exercise, and how sport and physical activities promote health from cellular to the whole body perspectives. The study of sports science traditionally incorporates areas of physiology (exercise physiology), psychology (sport psychology), anatomy, biomechanics, biochemistry and biokinetics.

Sports scientists and performance consultants are growing in demand and employment numbers, with the ever-increasing focus within the sporting world on achieving the best results possible. Through the study of science and sport, researchers have developed a greater understanding of how the human body reacts to exercise, training, different environments and many other stimuli. The mature disciplines and developing scientific research institutions have laid a solid foundation for sport science research.

体育科学又被称为运动科学，是研究健康的人体在体育锻炼中如何运转，并从细胞到整个人体的角度研究体育运动如何促进人体健康的一门学科。该学科涵盖众多研究领域，一般包括生理学（运动生理学）、心理学（运动心理学）、解剖学、生物力学、生物化学和生物运动学等。

目前体育界对体育成绩的关注越来越高，因此，对运动科学专家及成绩顾问的需求不断增长，该领域从业人员数量也不断增加。通过对科学与运动的研究，研究人员对于人体如何对体育运动、体育训练、不同外界环境与刺激因素之间的相互作用关系有了更深入的理解。目前，学科的成熟和科研机构的完善，又为体育科学研究奠定了坚实的基础。

Part Two — Reading

Physical Literacy: Teaching Children the ABCs of Movement

Rebecca A. Battista, Ph.D., FACSM

1 It is well documented that most youth are not meeting the current recommendations of 60 minutes of physical activity per day. Similar to teaching children the ABCs, it is important for kids to learn how to move and lead an active lifestyle. Just like the goal of teaching children to read and write allows them to explore the world, teaching them to move provides them with the ability to be active for life.

2 The concept of physical literacy is relatively new, but it is gaining much attention. Physical literacy is defined as "the motivation, confidence, physical competence, knowledge and understanding to value and take responsibility for engagement in physical activities for life". Physical literacy highlights the development of basic motor skills throughout childhood and suggests these skills form a foundation for future sport and/or physical activity participation. Think of literacy as it relates to reading and writing—these are essential skills children need to learn in order to be successful. Physical literacy is similar because it relates to acquiring important movement skills that will assist children in being active throughout life. These movement skills are things like walking, running, skipping, hopping, catching, throwing—all of which are considered fundamental movement skills. In other words, fundamental movement skills are the ABCs of future movements!

3 Fundamental movement skills can be broken down into locomotor skills and object control skills. Locomotor skills include movements like running, jumping, hopping, skipping and galloping. Object control skills include throwing, kicking, catching and striking. Most children (about 60 percent) should be proficient in these skills by ages five to six years. When children become proficient at basic movement skills, they can continue to add to their skill development and continue participating in many forms of physical activity. These forms of physical activity may include sports (e.g. soccer, baseball) or leisure time physical activities (e.g. walking, hiking). When these skills are not well developed, children may not want to participate in physical activities.

4 Recent campaigns and initiatives like "Designed to Move", "Let's Move!" and "Project Play" have emphasized the importance of creating positive physical activity experiences with children and focusing on basic movement skills. Providing opportunities for children to practice these movement skills, with both structured and unstructured play, is critical. Children need both opportunities and education on the basic skills. The focus should be on developing children's confidence in their skills, allowing them to participate in more activities and ultimately lead a more active lifestyle. It doesn't have to be hard to incorporate more physical activity into a child's life—it can be as simple as a family walk after dinner, going to the park or turning off the screens for an hour to play outside.

Word Bank

literacy	[ˈlɪtərəsi]	n. 读写能力；精通文学；素养
document	[ˈdɑːkjumənt]	v. 用文件证明
recommendation	[ˌrekəmenˈdeɪʃn]	n. 推荐；建议
motivation	[ˌmoʊtɪˈveɪʃn]	n. 动机；积极性；推动
competence	[ˈkɑːmpɪtəns]	n. 能力，胜任
highlight	[ˈhaɪlaɪt]	v. 使突出；强调
foundation	[faʊnˈdeɪʃn]	n. 基础；地基
essential	[ɪˈsenʃl]	adj. 基本的；必要的；精华的
skipping	[ˈskɪpɪŋ roʊp]	n. 跳绳
hopping	[ˈhɑːpɪŋ]	n. 单足跳跃
locomotor	[ˌloʊkəˈmoʊtə]	adj. 移动的，运动的
galloping	[ˈgæləpɪŋ]	n. 飞驰
striking	[ˈstraɪkɪŋ]	n. 击打
hiking	[ˈhaɪkɪŋ]	n. 徒步
campaign	[kæmˈpeɪn]	n. 运动；活动
critical	[ˈkrɪtɪkl]	adj. 决定性的
ultimately	[ˈʌltɪmətli]	adv. 最后；根本；基本上

Phrases

physical activity	身体活动，体育活动；体力活动
physical literacy	身体素质
assist in	（在某项任务中）有助于
turn off	关掉，关闭；拐弯，使转变方向

Unit 7
Sports Science

Task 1 Text Organization

Read the text and fill in the blanks.

Paragraphs	Main Idea	Supporting Details
Beginning (Para. 1)	Big problem: _____ _____ _____	• Two metaphors: (1) Similar to _____, it is important for kids to _____. (2) Just like _____ teaching them to _____.
Body (Paras. 2–3)	What is physical literacy? _____ _____ _____.	• Physical literacy highlights _____. • Fundamental movement skills can be broken down into _____. • When children become proficient at basic movement skills, _____.
End (Para. 4)	What should children do in physical activities? They should focus on _____.	The focus should be _____.

Task 2 Reading Comprehension

Exercise 1

Read the text and decide whether the following statements are true (T) or false (F).

1. _____ Think of literacy as it relates to reading and writing—these are essential skills children need to learn in order to be successful.
2. _____ In other words, fundamental movement skills are different from the ABCs of future movements!
3. _____ Locomotor skills include movements like running, jumping, hopping, skipping and galloping.
4. _____ Most children (about 60 percent) should be proficient in these skills by age three to five years.
5. _____ It has to be hard to incorporate more physical activity into a child's life.

93

Exercise 2

Read the text and answer the following questions.

1. What are the current recommendations of physical activity per day for children?
2. What is physical literacy according to the text?
3. What does physical literacy highlight?
4. What do locomotor skills include?
5. What do children need for the basic skills?

Task 3 Language in Use

Exercise 1

Match the underlined words or phrases in the left column with their corresponding meanings in the right column.

1. Most youth are not meeting the current <u>recommendations</u> of 60 minutes of physical activity per day.	A. move into the foreground to make more visible or prominent
2. Physical literacy <u>highlights</u> the development of basic motor skills throughout childhood.	B. moving
3. These skills form a <u>foundation</u> for future sport.	C. vitally necessary; basic; absolute
4. These are <u>essential</u> skills children need to learn in order to be successful.	D. push for something; express a good opinion of
5. Physical literacy is similar because it relates to acquiring important movement skills that will <u>assist</u> children in being active throughout life.	E. a series of action; a race
6. Fundamental movement skills can be broken down into <u>locomotor</u> skills and object control skills.	F. stop operating
7. Recent <u>campaigns</u> and initiatives like "Designed to Move" have emphasized the importance of creating positive physical activity experiences with children.	G. the basis on which something is grounded

8. Providing opportunities for children to practice these movement skills, with both structured and unstructured play, is critical.

H. give help or assistance

9. The focus should be on developing children's confidence in their skills, allowing them to participate in more activities and ultimately lead a more active lifestyle.

I. urgently needed; absolutely necessary

10. It can be as simple as a family walk after dinner, going to the park or turning off the screens for an hour to play outside.

J. furthest or highest degree or order

Exercise 2

Select one word for each blank from a list of choices given below.

| motivation | engagement | fundamental | foundation | throughout |
| literacy | relatively | highlights | essential | participation |

The concept of physical literacy is 1._____ new, but it is gaining much attention. Physical literacy is defined as "the 2._____, confidence, physical competence, knowledge and understanding to value and take responsibility for 3._____ in physical activities for life". Physical literacy 4._____ the development of basic motor skills throughout childhood and suggests these skills form a 5._____ for future sport and/or physical activity 6._____. Think of literacy as it relates to reading and writing—these are 7._____ skills children need to learn in order to be successful. Physical 8._____ is similar because it relates to acquiring important movement skills that will assist children in being active 9._____ life. These movement skills are things like walking, running, skipping, hopping, catching, throwing—all of which are considered 10._____ movement skills. In other words, fundamental movement skills are the ABCs of future movements!

Exercise 3

Translate the following sentences into English.
1. 他的问题和我的大体相似。(similar to)
2. 就像这些植物一样，我们也会往前走，活下去。(just like)
3. 各方面都要考虑到。(consider)

4. 我会协助你解决任何突发事件和矛盾。(assist in)

5. 他们也学到控制自己的情绪是多么的重要。(critical)

Fruits & Veggies—Do You Eat Too Few?

Nancy Clark, M.S., RD

Feeling ashamed and embarrassed, many of my clients "confess" they eat too few fruits and vegetables. They totally understand that fruits and veggies are good for their health and better than vitamin pills, but they can't figure out how to enjoy them more often—or how to get inspired to learn to like them. Sound familiar? Maybe this article will help you boost your intake of these healthful foods.

I Know I Should Eat More Fruit for Snacks, But I Just Don't...

When hunger strikes, a piece of fruit is unlikely to be your snack of first choice because it is not very hearty. That is, calorie-dense apple pie with ice cream can easily be far more appealing than just an apple. For example, enjoy an apple (or grapes) with cheese, smear a banana with peanut butter or combine raisins with nuts. Would that boost the snack-appeal?

How Many Fruits/Veggies Are Enough?

Ideally, you should eat a fruit or vegetable at each meal. If you don't/won't/can't do that, at least eat a pile of veggies with dinner to compensate for no produce at the other meals. You could also create a loaded smoothie at breakfast that has enough fruit (and veggie) for the whole day.

Other suggestions include:

• Breakfast: a large banana on cereal; lots of berries in yogurt; a tall glass of orange juice;

• Lunch: extra tomato and spinach in a wrap; a big bowl of fruit salad; a large apple (with cheese) for dessert;

• Snacks: tart cherry, grape or blueberry juice; banana (with peanut butter); dates; dried pineapple; vegetable juice;

• Dinner: pre-dinner munchies: baby carrots (with hummus), cherry tomatoes; at dinner: big pile of cooked veggies; extra-large side salad.

The More You Eat the More Nutrients You Get.

Eight ounces of orange juice offers all the vitamin C you need for the day. So does one stalk of cooked broccoli and half a green pepper. Could you consume a taller glass of orange juice, a bigger pile of broccoli, or munch on a whole pepper (like you'd eat an apple)? You'd consume double the vitamin C—plus electrolytes and many other health-boosting compounds.

Don't Like Many Veggies?

Because fruits and vegetables offer similar nutrients, you can swap one for the other. That is, if you don't enjoy red tomatoes, at least try to have red strawberries, red apples or red peppers. In general, you want to consume a variety of colors of fruits and/or veggies—and enjoy a rainbow of health:

- Red: strawberries, apples, watermelon, tomato;
- Orange: oranges, mango, papaya, sweet potato;
- Yellow: pineapple, peaches, and summer squash;
- Blue/purple: blueberry, plums, eggplant, purple grapes;
- Green: kiwi, honeydew melon, green grapes, broccoli, spinach, kale, peppers;
- White: banana, onion, potato, cauliflower.

Word Bank

ashamed	[əˈʃeɪmd]	adj. 惭愧的，感到难为情的
embarrassed	[ɪmˈbærəst]	adj. 尴尬的；窘迫的
client	[ˈklaɪənt]	n. 客户；顾客
confess	[kənˈfes]	v. 承认；坦白；忏悔
boost	[buːst]	v. 促进，增加
hearty	[ˈhɑːrti]	adj. 丰盛的；衷心的
cereal	[ˈsɪriəl]	n. 谷类，谷物
spinach	[ˈspɪnɪtʃ]	n. 菠菜
wrap	[ræp]	n. 包裹物；覆盖物
broccoli	[ˈbrɑːkəli]	n. 西兰花
electrolyte	[ɪˈlektrəlaɪt]	n. 电解质
compound	[ˈkɑːmpaʊnd]	n. 混合物，化合物
nutrient	[ˈnuːtriənt]	n. 营养物
swap	[swɑːp]	v. 与……交换；以……作交换
papaya	[pəˈpaɪə]	n. 木瓜
kale	[keɪl]	n. [植] 羽衣甘蓝

Phrases

vitamin pill	维生素丸
figure out	解决；算出；想出
compensate for	弥补……；赔偿……

Critical Reading and Thinking

Read the text and decide whether the following statements are true (T) or false (F).

1. _____ Feeling ashamed and embarrassed, many of my clients agree that they eat too few fruits and vegetables.
2. _____ They don't understand that fruits and veggies are good for their health and better than vitamin pills, but they can figure out how to enjoy them more often—or how to get inspired to learn to like them.
3. _____ When hunger strikes, a piece of fruit is likely to be your snack of first choice because it is very hearty.
4. _____ You'd better eat a fruit or vegetable at each meal.
5. _____ If you can't do that, at least eat a pile of veggies with dinner to compensate for no produce at the other meals.
6. _____ You could also drink some juice at breakfast that has enough fruit (and veggie) for the whole day.
7. _____ "You'd consume double the vitamin C—plus electrolytes and many other health-boosting compounds." This means you will get enough nutrients.
8. _____ Because fruits and vegetables offer different nutrients, you cannot swap one for the other.
9. _____ If you don't enjoy tomatoes, try to have other veggies or fruits.
10. _____ In general, you want to consume a variety of colors of fruits and/or veggies—and gets good health.

Translation

Translate the following sentences into Chinese.

1. They totally understand that fruits and veggies are good for their health and better than vitamin pills, but they can't figure out how to enjoy them more often—or how to get inspired to learn to like them.
2. When hunger strikes, a piece of fruit is unlikely to be your snack of first choice because it is not very hearty.
3. You could also create a loaded smoothie at breakfast that has enough fruit (and veggies) for the whole day.
4. Eight ounces of orange juice offers all the vitamin C you need for the day.
5. Because fruits and vegetables offer similar nutrients, you can swap one for the other.

Part Three — Listening and Speaking

Task 1

Word Bank

crisis	['kraɪsɪs]	n. 危机；危险期
inactivity	[ˌɪnæk'tɪvəti]	n. 静止；不活泼
obesity	[oʊ'biːsəti]	n. 肥大，肥胖
psychological	[ˌsaɪkə'lɑːdʒɪkl]	adj. 心理的；心理学的
stress	[stres]	n. 压力
depression	[dɪ'preʃn]	n. 沮丧；抑郁；（经济）萧条

Listen to an interview with Dr. Kidman, a leading expert in youth sports, and answer the following questions.

1. According to Dr. Kidman, what are many children facing now?
2. What are the physical benefits for children who play sports?
3. What are the psychological benefits?
4. What are the social benefits?
5. What suggestions does Dr. Kidman make on how to choose a sport for children?

Task 2

Word Bank

maintain	[meɪn'teɪn]	v. 维持；继续
packaged	['pækɪdʒ]	adj. 包装过的
takeout	[aɪ'diːə]	adj. 外卖的
intake	['ɪnteɪk]	n. 摄取量
toxin	['tɑːksɪn]	n. 毒素
take charge of		接管；负责

Listen to a passage about healthy diet, and decide whether the following statements are true (T) or false (F).

1. _____ Diet can have a great effect on your mood and emotions.
2. _____ The typical Western diet helps to improve your mood and lower the risk for mental health problems.

3. _____ Cooking meals at home can help control what goes into your diet.

4. _____ Fried chicken is healthier than fish.

5. _____ You can find out what's in the packaged food by reading the label.

Task 3

Listen to the five sentences from the recording, repeat each sentence after it is spoken, and then write them down.

1. _____.
2. _____.
3. _____.
4. _____.
5. _____.

Part Four Writing

Invitation Letters

A letter of invitation serves as a formal request for the presence of an individual, a group of people or an organization at an event. Invitation letters are often distributed for graduation celebrations, birthdays, weddings, anniversary parties, and some other occasions. It could be printed on paper or sent via e-mail.

An invitation letter may be formal or informal. Formal ones usually use some sentence structures and even adopt fixed patterns, while sentences used in informal ones differ greatly even if they are complete sentences (See Sample 1 and Sample 2).

Information in a letter of invitation covers the host, the location of the event, time and date of the event and even the dress code desired at the event. The letter should also include details about the event, such as a person's age for a birthday celebration. "R.S.V.P" or "r.s.v.p" is put at the end when the host expects a quick reply from the guest, although replying to an invitation is a social convention.

Sample 1 A formal invitation letter

> Mr. John Doe
>
> requests the pleasure of the company of
>
> Mr. and Mrs. Willy Hodes
>
> at a dinner in honor of his daughter
>
> Mary Doe
>
> on the occasion of her 10th birthday
>
> on Tuesday, January 8th
>
> at seven o'clock
>
> at his home
>
> 735 Maple Lane
>
> Centerville, Kansas 12346
>
> R.S.V.P. 334-7955 by January 2nd

Sample 2 An informal invitation letter

Dear Janet,

　　We are having a party for our daughter, Elizabeth's 8th birthday on Friday, 18th at 6 p.m. at our home and we wonder if you and Stephen can come. Please say you can come as you are always our most precious friends!

　　To help us plan the food, could you let us know if you can come before Wednesday? Thanks.

Yours,

Rose and George

Follow-up Writing

Suppose you are the senior assistant to the Principal of Beijing Sport University. The Principal, Lin Haijun asks you to write a letter to invite Prof. Martin Bush, a world-renowned expert in children's sports, to give a keynote speech at the Third International Conference on Children's Health, which will be held in your university from 1st June to 3rd June, 2016.

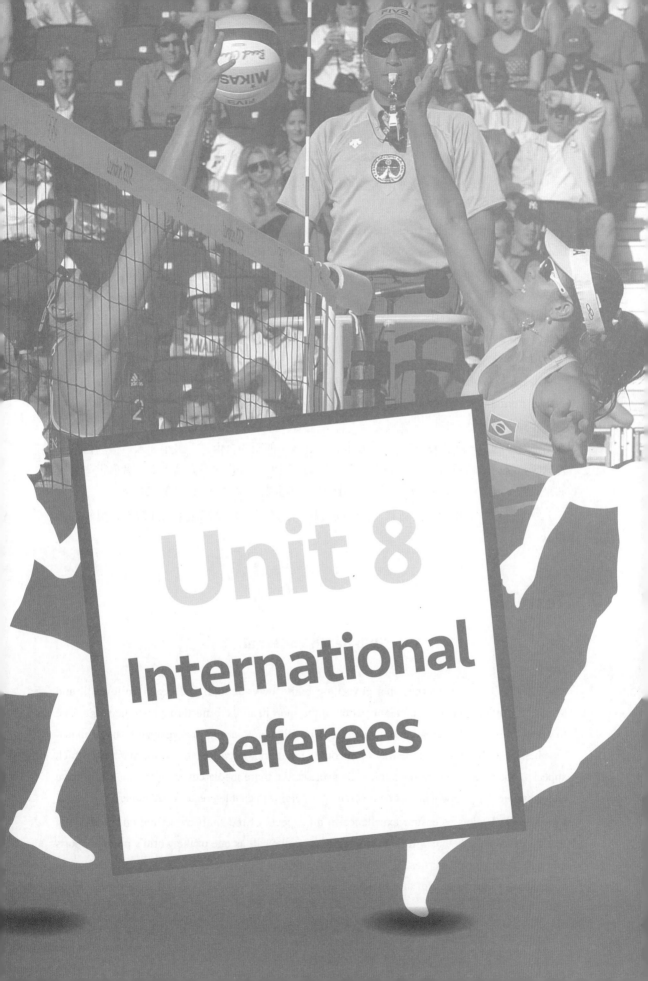

Unit 8
International Referees

Part One — Knowledge Preparation

The regulations, court sizes, the ball, the scoring system and exchange of the service in the Beach Volleyball regulations coincide partly with the volleyball match indoor. The playing court is a rectangle measuring 16 m×8 m, surrounded by a free zone, which is minimum of 3 m wide on all sides. There is no restriction for the service court and front and back rows. The match is won by the team that wins 2 sets. A set is won by the team which first scores 21 points with a minimum lead of two points. In the case of a 20−20 tie, play is continued until a two-point lead is achieved (22−20; 23−21; etc.).

Beach volleyball is strongly associated with a casual, beach-centric lifestyle. Fashion often extends from the clothing worn during play, like the bikini or board shorts.

沙滩排球的基本规则、场地大小、排球大小、得失分和交换发球权等方面与室内排球运动基本一样。场地为长方形，长 16 米，宽 8 米，四周为自由区，最小 3 米。但场内没有发球区和前后排的限制。一般采用 3 局 2 胜制，先得 21 分且比对方高出 2 分者赢得一局。如果双方打成 20 比 20 平分时，净胜 2 分一方才能获胜（如 22—20，23—21 等）。

沙滩排球一般比较轻松随意，且热闹有趣。打球时通常穿着比基尼和短裤，引领时尚潮流。

FIVB Beach Volleyball

The FIVB

1. The FIVB is the international governing body for volleyball and beach volleyball, and handles the management and communication of the sport in all its forms throughout the world. The FIVB has developed international competitions in collaboration with its organizers and affiliated members and set the rules in a way to encourage exciting, evenly-matched tournaments which appeal to sport fans. The more exciting the sport is, the more media coverage the sport will have and consequently, this will attract commercial partners, who enable greater prize money.

2. The FIVB aims to ensure excellence in all aspects of the sport by setting and preserving world-class standards that will maintain and grow volleyball as one of the world's premier sports and entertainment properties. It also aims to continue as part of the Olympic movement, in contributing to the success of the Olympic Games.

3 Furthermore, the FIVB is a global leader in innovative "new generation" of sports entertainment; with its solid, proven structure, the organization is perfectly placed to deliver its mission worldwide.

The Game

4 Beach volleyball is an Olympic discipline played outdoors, barefoot on a sand court with a ball, by teams of two people separated by a net. Beach volleyball was born on the Southern California beaches in the late 1920s and enjoyed a rapid international expansion thanks to the FIVB development programs, committed partners, promoters, hosting National Volleyball Federations, officials, and professional athletes, for the enjoyment of millions of fans and thousands of participating women's and men's players throughout the world. Beach volleyball is an outstanding, entertaining, healthy and drug-free sport, attracting upwardly mobile, affluent and fashion conscious audiences oriented towards an active lifestyle.

5 With its low cost to set up and play, it is ideal for development programs and "sport for-all" initiatives, as well as having an educational value being a non-contact sport, requiring an harmonious blend of body, will and mind-fitness, stamina, tactics and team play.

FIVB Beach Volleyball Competitions

6 International beach volleyball competitions, including professional and non-professional beach volleyball tournaments, are exclusive properties of the FIVB, directly under its authority. Promoters, together with the NFs, play an important role in ensuring the promotion and organization of each event locally.

7 The FIVB manages the following international beach volleyball competitions:

8 —FIVB Beach Volleyball World Championships: It is FIVB's elite competition held every four or two years depending on the received bids.

9 —FIVB Beach Volleyball World Tour: It is a professional beach volleyball circuit, where every season comprises the Grand Slam events, the Major events, the Open events, and the Season Final event.

10 —FIVB Beach Volleyball World Tour Season Final: It is held annually at the end of the season to determine the winner NF/team per gender of the FIVB Beach Volleyball World Tour. Starting from 2015 and onwards, the season will be completed after the FIVB World Tour Season Final, and a new season will start after the date of this event. This will create a momentum towards the FIVB World Tour Season Final. This implies that a season falls under two solar years. For instance, after the 2015 Season Final, the next season will be the 2015/2016, 2016/2017 and so on.

11 —Age Group World Championships (U-17, U-19 and U-21): They are held every two years for the young generation of athletes in three different age groups.

Word Bank

collaboration	[kəˌlæbəˈreɪʃn]	n. 合作
evenly	[ˈiːvnli]	adv. 平衡地；平坦地；平等地
coverage	[ˈkʌvərɪdʒ]	n. 新闻报道；覆盖范围
commercial	[kəˈmɜːrʃl]	adj. 商业的
property	[ˈprɑːpərti]	n. 财产；所有物
innovative	[ˈɪnəveɪtɪv]	adj. 创新的；革新的
expansion	[ɪkˈspænʃn]	n. 扩大；膨胀
committed	[kəˈmɪtɪd]	adj. 忠诚的；坚定的；献身于某种事业的
promoter	[prəˈmoʊtər]	n. 促进者；发起人
affluent	[ˈæfluənt]	adj. 富裕的
oriented	[ˈɔːrientɪd]	adj. 以……为方向的；以……为目的的
initiative	[ɪˈnɪʃətɪv]	n. 项目；首创精神；主动权
harmonious	[hɑːrˈmoʊniəs]	adj. 和谐的；和睦的；音调优美的
blend	[blend]	n. 混合物
exclusive	[ɪkˈskluːsɪv]	adj. 独占的；唯一的；排外的
bid	[bɪd]	n. 出价
circuit	[ˈsɜːrkɪt]	n. 巡回；线路；环形；电路，回路

Phrases

appeal to	吸引
contribute to	为……做贡献；是……的原因
fall under	被列为，归入……类
solar year	阳历

Proper Names

FIVB (International Volleyball Federation)	国际排球联合会
National Volleyball Federations	国家排球联合会
Beach Volleyball World Championships	世界沙滩排球锦标赛
Beach Volleyball World Tour	世界沙滩排球巡回赛
the Grand Slam events	大满贯赛
the Major events	重大赛事
the Open events	公开赛
the Season Final event	季赛决赛
Age Group World Championships (U-17, U-19 and U-21)	年龄组世界冠军赛（17 岁组，19 岁组，21 岁组）

Unit 8
International Referees

Task 1 Text Organization

Read the text and fill in the blanks.

Paragraphs	Key Words	Supporting Details
Beginning (Paras. 1–3)	The _____	• an international governing body for volleyball and _____ • handling the management and communication in all its forms: 　(1) developing _____ 　(2) _____ the rules • two aims: 　(1) ensuring _____ 　(2) _____ the success of the Olympics • the mission: 　innovating "_____" sports entertainment
Body (Paras. 4–5)	The Game	• an _____ discipline • birth: 　(1) on the _____ California beaches 　(2) in the _____ • an outstanding, _____, healthy and drug-free sport • orienting audience towards an active lifestyle
End (Paras. 6–11)	FIVB Beach Volleyball Competitions	• the two exclusive properties of FIVB: 　(1) _____ beach volleyball tournaments 　(2) _____ beach volleyball tournaments • two important organizers of local events: 　(1) _____ 　(2) the NFs • competitions managed by FIVB: 　(1) FIVB Beach Volleyball World Championships 　(2) FIVB Beach Volleyball World Tour 　　(the Grand Slam events, the Major events, the Open events, and the Season Final event) 　(3) Age Group World Championships (U-17, U-19 and U-21)

107

Task 2 Reading Comprehension

Exercise 1

Read the text and decide whether the following statements are true (T) or false (F).

1. _____ The FIVB is an international organization in charge of the management, communication and international competitions for volleyball and beach volleyball.
2. _____ The FIVB plays a world-leading role in the "new generation" of sports entertainment.
3. _____ Beach volleyball is not an Olympic sport yet.
4. _____ International beach volleyball competitions include only professional tournaments.
5. _____ The FIVB Beach Volleyball World Tour Season Final is a competition held every year to determine the winner NF/team per gender of the FIVB Beach Volleyball World Tour.

Exercise 2

Read the text and answer the following questions.

1. What is the aim of FIVB?
2. Why did beach volleyball expand rapidly since its birth in the late 1920s?
3. What kind of sport is beach volleyball?
4. What are the FIVB beach volleyball competitions?
5. What is the FIVB Beach Volleyball World Tour composed of?

Task 3 Language in Use

Exercise 1

Match the underlined words in the left column with their corresponding meanings in the right column.

1. With its solid, proven structure, the organization is perfectly placed to deliver its mission worldwide.   A. rich; prosperous

2. Beach Volleyball enjoyed a rapid international expansion.   B. contests to decide who is the champion

3. Beach volleyball attracts upwardly mobile, affluent and fashion-conscious audiences.   C. reliable; that can be depended on

4. The competitions include professional and non-professional beach volleyball tournaments.   D. (of sport, etc.) practiced as a full-time job

Unit 8
International Referees

5. The FIVB Beach Volleyball World <u>Championships</u> is held every four or two years.

6. The FIVB Beach Volleyball World Tour is a professional beach volleyball <u>circuit</u>.

7. This will create a <u>momentum</u> towards the FIVB World Tour Season Final.

8. The Age Group World Championships are held every two years for the young generation of <u>athletes</u> in three different age groups.

E. an impelling force or strength

F. action or state of becoming greater in size, number or importance

G. persons trained to compete in sports

H. series of matches in which the same players regularly take part in

Exercise 2

Select one word or phrase for each blank from a list of choices given below.

| commercial | innovative | appeal to | affiliated | premier |
| deliver | preserving | collaboration | consequently | tournaments |

The FIVB is the international governing body for volleyball and beach volleyball and handles the management and communication of the sport in all its forms throughout the world. The FIVB has developed international competitions in 1._____ with its organizers and 2._____ members and set the rules in a way to encourage exciting, evenly-matched 3._____ which 4._____ sport fans. The more exciting the sport is, the more media coverage the sport will have and 5._____, this will attract 6._____ partners, who enable greater prize money. FIVB aims to ensure excellence in all aspects of the sport by setting and 7._____ world-class standards that will maintain and grow volleyball as one of the world's 8._____ sports and entertainment properties. It also aims to continue as part of the Olympic movement, in contributing to the success of the Olympic Games. Furthermore, FIVB is a global leader in 9._____ "new generation" sports entertainment and with its solid, proven structure, the organization is perfectly placed to 10._____ its mission worldwide.

Exercise 3

Translate the following sentences into English.
1. 我们锻炼得越多，就会越健康。(the more..., the more...)
2. 奥运会每四年在不同的国家举办一次。(every... years)

3. 董事会由两名女性、七名男性成员组成。(comprise)
4. 这种疾病在全国到处传播，父母不得不将这个孩子和他的哥哥隔离开。(separate... from...)
5. 家庭教育对一个人的成功起着重要作用。(play a role in...)

Volleyball Comes Home to Copacabana

With Copacabana, the world's most iconic beach and the game's spiritual home, as the venue, beach volleyball players are preparing for a truly special race for gold.

Beach volleyball players have competed for Olympic gold in parks and on royal parade grounds, but at the Rio Games beach, volleyball will actually be played on a beach. After Sydney 2000, when the iconic Bondi beach was the venue, Rio 2016 is the second time for the volleyball tournament to take place on a genuine stretch of sand shared by sun worshippers and surfers.

The United States, having invented the game, can claim to be the home of beach volleyball, but its soul lives in Brazil, and Copacabana beach is the altar where they come to worship. The stretch of white sand watched over by the statue of Christ the Redeemer is probably the most famous beach in the world, making Copacabana the quintessential venue for the sport's showcase event.

Brazilian beach volleyball players will seek inspiration from one of the country's most vibrant venues as they attempt to end traditional American domination of the event at the Olympics. Brazilian female favorites Talita Antunes and Larissa Franca can bank on fervent fans at the Copacabana where the sport is an intrinsic part of Rio's coastal culture and does not require an Olympics to get an audience. But experienced American Kerri Walsh Jennings has topped the podium at the last three Olympics. This will be the first time the American has gone for gold on an actual beach.

"Playing in Copa is amazing. The energy is electric and it absolutely does elevate the play. It is going to be amazing to play in front of such crazy, passionate fans. It is something we all relish," she said.

Whatever happens this time, everyone agrees on one thing: Copacabana is the most incredible volleyball venue in the Olympic history. While the athletes will be focusing on the serious business in Rio, the fans are braced for an Olympic beach party, with the action starting early in the day and running late into the evening. With the samba and pounding surf providing a sunny soundtrack, beach volleyball is one of the hottest tickets in town.

And for Brazilian contestants like Pedro Solberg, the sandy venue is particularly special, "It's a unique opportunity in my life. I just want to enjoy this moment and have fun."

Unit 8
International Referees

Word Bank

venue	['venjuː]	n. 场所
altar	['ɔːltər]	n. 祭坛，圣坛
vibrant	['vaɪbrənt]	adj. 振动的；响亮的；充满生气的
fervent	['fɜːrvənt]	adj. 炽热的；强烈的；热诚的
intrinsic	[ɪn'trɪnsɪk]	adj. 固有的，内在的，本质的
podium	['poʊdiəm]	n. 领奖台
electric	[ɪ'lektrɪk]	adj. 令人激动的；电的，带电的
elevate	['elɪveɪt]	v. 提高，提升；鼓舞
passionate	['pæʃənət]	adj. 激昂的，热烈的
relish	['relɪʃ]	v. 盼望，期待；欣赏；品尝
brace	[breɪs]	v. 支撑；准备

Phrase

bank on	寄希望于

Critical Reading and Thinking

Read the text and decide whether the following statements are true (T) or false (F).

1. _____ Bondi beach was the venue for Beach Volleyball at the 2000 Sydney Olympics.
2. _____ America invented Beach Volleyball, but the soul of it is still in Brazil.
3. _____ The statue of Christ the Redeemer in America is probably the most famous beach in the world.
4. _____ Almost all the Rios love the sport of Beach Volleyball because of Rio's coastal culture.
5. _____ Kerri Walsh Jennings is the first American who has gone for the gold on an actual beach.
6. _____ Playing in Copa is not only amazing, but also electric.
7. _____ Beach volleyball players can elevate the play at the Copacabana.
8. _____ Copacabana is the most incredible volleyball venue in the Olympic history.
9. _____ Because the Olympic beach party usually starts early in the day and runs late into the evening, several matches are scheduled for a midnight start.
10. _____ For Brazilian contestants like Pedro Solberg, the sandy venue is something special.

Translation

Translate the following sentences into Chinese.

1. With Copacabana, the world's most iconic beach and the game's spiritual home, as the venue, beach volleyball players are preparing for a truly special race for gold.

2. After Sydney 2000, when the iconic Bondi Beach was the venue, Rio 2016 is the second time for the volleyball tournament to take place on a genuine stretch of sand shared by sun worshippers and surfers.

3. The United States, having invented the game, can claim to be the home of beach volleyball, but its soul lives in Brazil, and Copacabana beach is the altar where they come to worship.

4. Brazilian beach volleyball players will seek inspiration from one of the country's most vibrant venues as they attempt to end traditional American domination of the event at the Olympics.

5. Whatever happens this time, everyone agrees on one thing: Copacabana is the most incredible volleyball venue in the Olympic history.

Part Three Listening and Speaking

Task 1

Word Bank

register	['redʒɪstər]	v. 登记，注册
intermediate	[ˌɪntər'miːdiət]	adj. 中间的，中级的
promote	[prə'moʊt]	v. 使（学生）升级
reasonable	['riːznəbl]	adj. 合理的，公道的
fee	[fiː]	n. 费，费用
refund	['riːfʌnd]	n. 退款
apply	[ə'plaɪ]	v. 涂，敷（药）
sunscreen	['sʌnskriːn]	n. 防晒霜

Listen to a telephone conversation between a caller and a receptionist of the Beach Volleyball Club and answer the following questions.

1. How many levels of courses does the Beach Volleyball Club offer?

2. Which level of course will the caller probably choose to register for?

3. How much does it cost?

4. Can the caller get a refund if he is unable to attend the course?

5. What does the receptionist suggest the caller wear to the class?

Task 2

Word Bank

responsible	[rɪˈspɑːnsəbl]	*adj.* 负责的，可靠的；有责任的
shot	[ʃɑːt]	*n.* 击球
volley	[ˈvɑːli]	*n.* (球着地前的) 截击，拦击
strengthen	[ˈstreŋθn]	*v.* 加强；巩固

Listen to a passage about beach volleyball and choose the best answer to each question.

1. According to the speaker, beach volleyball can be played with as few as_____.

   A. two people   B. four people

   C. six people   D. eight people

2. When you join a larger beach volleyball team, you'll_____.

   A. have as many shots as possible   B. improve your volleyball skills

   C. be responsible for less ground   D. do more running

3. Why is it much slower to play beach volleyball than regular volleyball?

   A. Because the beach volleyball is heavier.

   B. Because the rules are different.

   C. Because it is usually a larger team.

   D. Because it is harder to move quickly on sand.

4. What does the writer think of beach volleyball?

   A. It is exciting and fun.   B. It is dangerous.

   C. It needs less power.   D. It is difficult to learn.

Task 3

Listen to the five sentences from the recording, repeat each sentence after it is spoken, and then write them down.

1. _____.
2. _____.
3. _____.
4. _____.
5. _____.

Reply to Invitation Letters

It is social etiquette to give a quick reply to an invitation letter to express gratitude, no matter if it is an acceptance or decline. A reply to accept an invitation usually expresses thanks, informs the host of the invitee's attendance, and also confirms the time and location of the event. To refuse an invitation politely, a reply makes an apology and offers the reason. Wishes can be expressed at the end of a reply declining an invitation.

The tone used in a reply letter should be the same as that used in the invitation letter, that is to say, a formal tone should be used in reply to a formal invitation, and an informal tone should be used in reply to an informal one.

The following are sample replies to the sample invitation letters in Unit 7.

Sample 1   An acceptance to a formal invitation

Mr. and Mrs. Willy Hodes
accept with pleasure the kind invitation of
Mr. John Doe
to a dinner in honor of his daughter
Mary Doe
on the occasion of her 10th birthday
on Tuesday, January 8th
at seven o'clock
at his home
735 Maple Lane
Centerville, Kansas 12346

Sample 2 A refusal to a formal invitation

> Mr. and Mrs. Willy Hodes
> regret that
> owning to a previous engagement
> they cannot accept the generous invitation of
> Mr. John Doe
> to a dinner in honor of his daughter
> Mary Doe
> on the occasion of her 10th birthday
> on Tuesday, January 8th
> at seven o'clock
> at his home
> 735 Maple Lane
> Centerville, Kansas 12346

Sample 3 An acceptance to an informal invitation

Dear Rose and George,

    Thank you for your kind invitation to Elizabeth's birthday party on Friday, 18th at 6 p.m. We shall be very happy indeed to come and help you on Tuesday. Look forward to seeing you then.

Best wishes,

Janet

Sample 4   A refusal to an informal invitation

Dear Rose and George,

Thank you so much for inviting me to Elizabeth's birthday party. Unfortunately, I will be on a business trip for that night, so I won't be able to attend. I hope you have a wonderful time celebrating this special occasion.

Your pal,
Janet

Follow-up Writing

Write two reply letters to the invitation letter you have written in Unit 7 with an appropriate tone. One expresses Prof. Martin Bush's acceptance and another decline.

Glossary

abandon	[ə'bændən]	adj. 放弃；放任	U6TB
accessibility	[əkˌsesə'bɪləti]	n. 可以得到；易接近	U4TA
acclaim	[ə'kleɪm]	n. 欢呼，喝彩；称赞	U6TA
accumulate	[ə'kjuːmjəleɪt]	v. 积攒，积累	U3TA
acupuncture	['ækjupʌŋktʃər]	n. 针刺；[中医] 针刺疗法	U5TB
administration	[ədˌmɪnɪ'streɪʃn]	n. 管理；行政；实施；行政机构	U1TA
aerobic	[e'roʊbɪk]	adj. 需氧的；有氧健身的	U3TB
aerobics	[e'roʊbɪks]	n. 有氧运动法；健美操	U5TA
affiliated	[ə'fɪlieɪtɪd]	adj. 附属的；有关联的	U1TA
affluent	['æfluənt]	adj. 富裕的	U8TA
agility	[ə'dʒɪləti]	n. 敏捷，灵活；机敏	U2TA
alignment	[ə'laɪnmənt]	n. 校准	U5TB
all-around	[ˌɔːl ə'raʊnd]	adj. 全面的；综合性的	U2TA
altar	['ɔːltər]	n. 祭坛，圣坛	U8TB
ambassador	[æm'bæsədər]	n. 大使；代表；使节	U2TA
ample	['æmp(ə)l]	adj. 丰富的；足够的；宽敞的	U6TB
anchor	['æŋkər]	n. 锚；依靠；新闻节目主播 v. 抛锚；停泊；用锚系住；担任（广播电视新闻节目）的主持人	U4TA
animate	['ænɪmeɪt]	v. 使有生气；使活泼	U5TB
appoint	[ə'pɔɪnt]	v. 任命，指定；约定	U1TA
approach	[ə'proʊtʃ]	n. 方法；途径	U5TA
approximately	[ə'prɑːksɪmətli]	adv. 大约，近似地，近于	U3TB
archery	['ɑːtʃəri]	n. 箭术，射箭	U6TB
arena	[ə'riːnə]	n. 竞技场	U4TA
aristocrat	[ə'rɪstəkræt]	n. 贵族	U6TA
artificial	[ˌɑːrtɪ'fɪʃl]	adj. 人造的；虚伪的；武断的	U4TA
ascent	[ə'sent]	n. 上升；上坡路；晋升，提升	U4TA

117

ashamed	[əˈʃeɪmd]	adj. 惭愧的，感到难为情的	U7TB
assemble	[əˈsembl]	v. 集合，聚集	U1TA
astonish	[əˈstɑːnɪʃ]	v. 惊讶	U6TA
attain	[əˈteɪn]	v. 实现；获得；达到	U4TA
atypical	[ˌeɪˈtɪpɪkl]	adj. 不合规则的；非典型的	U2TB
avenue	[ˈævənuː]	n.（比喻达到某物的）途径，手段	U5TB
avowed	[əˈvaʊd]	adj. 公开宣布的；公开承认的	U5TB
awesome	[ˈɔːsəm]	adj. 令人敬畏的；可怕的；极好的	U2TA
ballot	[ˈbælət]	n. 投票；投票总数	U2TB
bent	[bent]	adj. 弯曲的	U3TA
bid	[bɪd]	n. 出价	U8TA
blend	[blend]	n. 混合物	U8TA
block	[blɑːk]	v. 阻止；阻塞；限制；封盖	U2TA
bolt	[boʊlt]	n. 门闩；螺栓 v.（突然）逃离；闩住；狼吞虎咽 adv. 挺直地	U4TA
boost	[buːst]	v. 促进，增加	U7TB
bouldering	[ˈboʊldərɪŋ]	n. 抱石攀岩运动	U4TA
boundary	[ˈbaʊndri]	n. 边界；范围；分界线	U3TA
brace	[breɪs]	v. 支撑；准备	U8TB
broccoli	[ˈbrɑːkəli]	n. 西兰花	U7TB
bunker	[ˈbʌŋkər]	n. [高尔夫] 沙坑；[军事] 掩蔽壕；煤仓	U4TB
buttock	[ˈbʌtək]	n. 臀部	U3TB
camming	[ˈkæmɪŋ]	n. 凸轮系统	U4TA
campaign	[kæmˈpeɪn]	n. 运动；活动	U7TA
capture	[ˈkæptʃə]	v. 捕捉；获得	U6TA
Catholicism	[kəˈθɑːləsɪzəm]	n. 天主教	U2TA
caution	[ˈkɔːʃn]	v. 警告	U3TA
celebrity	[səˈlebrəti]	n. 名人	U1TB
cereal	[ˈsɪriəl]	n. 谷类，谷物	U7TB
charity	[ˈtʃærəti]	n. 慈善；施舍；慈善团体	U1TB
chock	[ˌtʃɑːk]	n. 楔子，木楔，楔形木垫 v. 用楔子垫阻 adv. 紧紧地	U4TA
circuit	[ˈsɜːrkɪt]	n. 巡回；线路；环形；电路，回路	U8TA

client	[ˈklaɪənt]	n. 客户；顾客	U7TB
clip	[klɪp]	v. 夹住；剪短；疾驰；猛击 n. 夹子；回形针；钳；修剪；(羊毛的)剪下量	U4TA
coach	[koʊtʃ]	n. 教练 v. 训练，执教	U1TB
collaboration	[kə͵læbəˈreɪʃn]	n. 合作	U8TA
combat	[ˈkɑːmbæt]	n. 战斗；争论	U5TB
commence	[kəˈmens]	v. 开始；着手	U1TA
commercial	[kəˈmɜːrʃl]	adj. 商业的	U8TA
commissioner	[kəˈmɪʃənər]	n. 理事；委员；行政长官；总裁	U2TB
committed	[kəˈmɪtɪd]	adj. 忠诚的；坚定的；献身于某种事业的	U8TA
competence	[ˈkɑːmpɪtəns]	n. 能力，胜任	U7TA
complementary	[͵kɑmplɪˈmentri]	adj. 补足的，补充的	U5TB
comply	[kəmˈplaɪ]	v. 遵守；顺从，遵从；答应	U2TA
compound	[ˈkɑːmpaʊnd]	n. 混合物，化合物	U7TB
comprise	[kəmˈpraɪz]	v. 包含，由……组成	U1TA
conceive	[kənˈsiːv]	v. 构思；怀孕	U2TB
confess	[kənˈfes]	v. 承认；坦白；忏悔	U7TB
connotation	[͵kɑːnəˈteɪʃn]	n. 内涵；隐含意义	U6TB
conquer	[ˈkɑːŋkər]	v. 征服，克服；战胜，得胜	U4TA
consciously	[ˈkɑːnʃəsli]	adv. 自觉地；有意识地	U3TB
conventional	[kənˈvenʃənl]	adj. 传统的；惯例的；常规的	U4TB
coolie	[ˈkuːli]	n. (印度的)苦力；小工	U5TA
corruption	[kəˈrʌpʃn]	n. 贪污，腐败；堕落	U1TA
counterpart	[ˈkaʊntərpɑːrt]	n. 对应的人或物	U1TB
coverage	[ˈkʌvərɪdʒ]	n. 新闻报道；覆盖范围	U8TA
crag	[kræg]	n. 峭壁，危岩	U4TA
critical	[ˈkrɪtɪkl]	adj. 决定性的	U7TA
debut	[deɪˈbjuː]	v. 初次登台	U2TB
decadent	[ˈdekədənt]	adj. 颓废的	U5TA
decline	[dɪˈklaɪn]	n. 下降；衰退	U6TA
dedication	[͵dedɪˈkeɪʃn]	n. 奉献；献身	U6TA
defined	[dɪˈfaɪnd]	adj. 有定义的，确定的；清晰的	U3TB
descent	[dɪˈsent]	n. 下降；下坡；家世；血统；衰落；继承	U4TA

dictate	['dɪkteɪt]	v. 命令，规定；口述；使听写	U3TA
discipline	['dɪsəplɪn]	n. 训练；学科；项目；纪律	U3TB
discrimination	[dɪˌskrɪmɪ'neɪʃn]	n. 歧视	U1TB
disqualified	[dɪs'kwɑːlɪfaɪd]	adj. 不合格的；被取消资格的	U3TA
diverse	[daɪ'vɜːrs]	adj. 不同的；多种多样的	U1TB
division	[dɪ'vɪʒn]	n. [体] 赛区；除法；部门；分割	U2TA
document	['dɑːkjumənt]	v. 用文件证明	U7TA
drag	[dræg]	v. 拖累；拖拉	U6TB
dribbling	['drɪbl]	n. 控球；漏泄	U2TB
duplicate	['duːplɪkeɪt]	v. 复制；使加倍	U2TA
elbow	['elboʊ]	n. 肘	U3TB
electric	[ɪ'lektrɪk]	adj. 令人激动的；电的，带电的	U8TB
electrolyte	[ɪ'lektrəlaɪt]	n. 电解质	U7TB
elevate	['elɪveɪt]	v. 提高，提升；鼓舞	U8TB
embarrassed	[ɪm'bærəst]	adj. 尴尬的；窘迫的	U7TB
emerge	[i'mɜːrdʒ]	v. 出现，显现，浮现	U1TB
emulate	['emjuleɪt]	v. 模仿，效仿	U2TA
endeavor	[ɪn'devər]	n. 尽力，竭力	U6TA
endpoint	['endˌpɔɪnt]	n. 端点	U4TA
endurance	[ɪn'dʊrəns]	n. 忍耐，忍耐力；耐性	U4TA
enhance	[ɪn'hæns]	v. 提高；加强	U5TB
essential	[ɪ'senʃl]	adj. 基本的；必要的；精华的	U7TA
evenly	['iːvnli]	adv. 平衡地；平坦地；平等地	U8TB
exclusive	[ɪk'skluːsɪv]	adj. 独占的；唯一的；排外的	U8TA
expansion	[ɪk'spænʃn]	n. 扩大；膨胀	U8TA
fad	[fæd]	n. 时尚；一时的爱好；一时流行的狂热	U6TB
fairway	['ferweɪ]	n.（高尔夫球）球道；航路；开阔的通道	U4TB
fame	[feɪm]	n. 名声，名望	U6TA
fanfare	['fænfer]	n. 喇叭或号角嘹亮的吹奏声；吹牛，炫耀	U2TB
featured	['fiːtʃərd]	adj. 特定的；被作为特色的	U2TB
fervent	['fɜːrvənt]	adj. 炽热的；强烈的；热诚的	U8TB
fiercely	['fɪrsli]	adv. 猛烈地，激烈地	U1TB
flourish	['flɜːrɪʃ]	v. 兴旺；活跃	U5TA

formation	[fɔːrˈmeɪʃn]	n. 构造；[地]地层；形成；队形	U4TA
fossil	[ˈfɔsəl]	n. 化石；僵化的事物；顽固不化的人	
		adj. 化石的；陈腐的，守旧的	U6TB
foundation	[faʊnˈdeɪʃn]	n. 基础；地基	U7TA
freak	[friːk]	n. 怪人；怪事	U2TA
gale	[geɪl]	n. 狂风；一阵（喧闹，笑声等）	U4TB
galloping	[ˈgæləpɪŋ]	n. 飞驰	U7TA
gear	[gɪr]	n. 传动装置；齿轮；排挡；工具，装备	
		v. 调整，使适应于；以齿轮连起	U4TA
generate	[ˈdʒenəreɪt]	v. 生成，产生，发生	U1TA
genesis	[ˈdʒenəsɪs]	n. 发生；起源	U5TB
globalization	[ˌgloʊbələˈzeɪʃn]	n. 全球化	U1TB
guru	[ˈguruː]	n. 古鲁（指印度教等宗教的宗师或领袖）；	
		领袖；专家	U4TB
hamstring	[ˈhæmstrɪŋ]	n. 肌腱；蹄筋	U3TB
handicapper	[ˈhændɪˌkæpə]	n. 裁判人员；（赛马等时）决定优劣条件之人	U4TB
harmonious	[hɑːrˈmoʊniəs]	adj. 和谐的；和睦的；音调优美的	U8TA
hassle	[ˈhæsl]	n. 困难；争吵；麻烦 v. 烦扰；麻烦	U4TA
hazard	[ˈhæzərd]	n. 危险；冒险；危害	U4TB
headquarter	[ˈhedˈkwɔːtə]	v. 在……设总部	U1TA
hearty	[ˈhɑːrti]	adj. 丰盛的；衷心的	U7TB
heritage	[ˈherɪtɪdʒ]	n. 遗产；传统；继承物	U5TA
highlight	[ˈhaɪlaɪt]	v. 使突出；强调	U7TA
hiking	[ˈhaɪkɪŋ]	n. 徒步	U7TA
hopping	[ˈhɑːpɪŋ]	n. 单足跳跃	U7TA
host	[hoʊst]	v. 主持；当主人招待	U1TA
iconic	[aɪˈkɑːnɪk]	adj. 偶像的；图标的	U1TB
iliopsoas	[ɪlɪoʊˈsoʊrs]	n. [解剖]髂腰肌	U3TB
illiteracy	[ɪˈlɪtərəsi]	n. 文盲；无知	U2TA
imperial	[ɪmˈpɪriəl]	adj. 帝国的；皇帝的	U6TB
implementation	[ˌɪmplɪmenˈteɪʃn]	n. 执行，履行；实现	U1TA
infraction	[ɪnˈfrækʃn]	n. 违反	U3TA
initiative	[ɪˈnɪʃətɪv]	n. 项目；首创精神；主动权	U8TA

innovative	[ˈɪnəveɪtɪv]	adj. 创新的；革新的	U8TA
interval	[ˈɪntərvl]	n. 间隔，间距；幕间休息	U1TA
intrinsic	[ɪnˈtrɪnsɪk]	adj. 固有的，内在的，本质的	U8TB
Islam	[ˈɪzlɑːm]	n. 伊斯兰教	U2TA
kale	[keɪl]	n. [植] 羽衣甘蓝	U7TB
label	[ˈleɪbl]	v. 贴标签于；标注	U2TA
languish	[ˈlæŋgwɪʃ]	v. 凋萎；失去活力	U6TB
lean	[liːn]	v. 倚靠	U3TB
legacy	[ˈlegəsi]	n. 遗产	U5TA
lineup	[ˈlaɪn ʌp]	n. 阵容；一组人	U2TB
literacy	[ˈlɪtərəsi]	n. 读写能力；精通文学；素养	U7TA
local	[ˈloʊkl]	adj. 当地的；局部的；地方性的	U3TA
locomotor	[ˌloʊkəˈmoʊtə]	adj. 移动的，运动的	U7TA
massive	[ˈmæsɪv]	adj. 大量的；巨大的，厚重的；魁伟的	U6TA
medalist	[ˈmedəlɪst]	n. 奖牌获得者	U6TA
meditation	[ˌmedɪˈteɪʃn]	n. 冥想；沉思	U5TB
minority	[maɪˈnɔːrəti]	n. 少数民族；少数派	U5TA
motivation	[ˌmoʊtɪˈveɪʃn]	n. 动机；积极性；推动	U7TA
multiple	[ˈmʌltɪpl]	adj. 多样的；许多的	U5TA
nationalist	[ˈnæʃnəlɪst]	adj. 民族主义的；国家主义的	U6TB
notably	[ˈnoʊtəbli]	adv. 显著地；尤其	U1TA
nutrient	[ˈnuːtriənt]	n. 营养物	U7TB
objective	[əbˈdʒektɪv]	adj. 客观的；真实的 n. 目标；目的	U4TA
obstacle	[ˈɑːbstəkl]	n. 障碍；绊脚石	U4TA
oriental	[ˌɔːriˈentl]	adj. 东方的；东方人的	U5TB
oriented	[ˈɔːrientɪd]	adj. 以……为方向的；以……为目的的	U8TA
origin	[ˈɔːrɪdʒɪn]	n. 起源，开端	U6TA
outnumber	[ˌaʊtˈnʌmbər]	v. 数目超过；比……多	U1TB
ovation	[oʊˈveɪʃn]	n. 热烈欢迎；大喝彩	U6TA
oversee	[ˌoʊvərˈsiː]	v. 监督；审查	U1TA
papaya	[pəˈpaɪə]	n. 木瓜	U7TB
par	[pɑr]	n. 标准杆；标准；票面价值；平均数量 adj. 标准的；票面的	U4TB

单词	音标	释义	位置
passion	['pæʃn]	n. 激情；热情；酷爱	U1TB
passionate	['pæʃənət]	adj. 激昂的，热烈的	U8TB
perish	['perɪʃ]	v. 死亡；毁灭	U6TB
perpetual	[pər'petʃuəl]	adj. 永久的；永恒的	U5TB
philosophy	[fə'lɑsəfi]	n. 哲学；哲理	U5TB
pit	[pɪt]	v. 使竞争；窖藏；使凹下	U2TB
pitch	[pɪtʃ]	n. 足球场	U1TB
pivot	['pɪvət]	v. 在枢轴上转动；随……转移	U3TB
playoff	['pleɪɔːf]	n. 季后赛；复赛	U2TA
pliable	['plaɪəbl]	adj. 柔韧的；柔软的	U5TB
podium	['poʊdiəm]	n. 领奖台	U8TB
popliteal	[pɒp'lɪtɪrl]	adj. 膝后窝的	U3TB
posture	['pɑːstʃər]	n. 姿势；态度；情形	U3TB
practitioner	[præk'tɪʃənər]	n. 从业者	U5TB
premiere	[prɪ'mɪr]	n. 首映式；首映	U5TA
principally	['prɪnsəpli]	adv. 主要地；大部分	U3TB
prohibition	[ˌproʊə'bɪʃn]	n. 禁止；禁令；禁酒	U2TB
promoter	[prə'moʊtər]	n. 促进者；发起人	U8TA
promotion	[prə'moʊʃn]	n. 推广，晋升；推销，促销；促进；发扬，振兴	U1TA
property	['prɑːpərti]	n. 财产；所有物	U8TA
prospective	[prə'spektɪv]	adj. 未来的；预期的	U3TB
publicity	[pʌb'lɪsəti]	n. 宣传，宣扬；公开；广告	U2TB
pyrotechnics	[ˌpaɪrə'teknɪks]	n. 烟火制造术；各种烟火	U2TB
quintessential	[ˌkwɪntɪ'senʃl]	adj. 精髓的，精粹的	U1TB
racial	['reɪʃl]	adj. 种族的；人种的	U5TA
racism	['reɪsɪzəm]	n. 种族主义，种族歧视；人种偏见	U1TB
rear	[rɪr]	adj. 后方的；后面的	U3TA
recognizable	['rekəgnaɪzəbl]	adj. 可辨认的；可认出的	U5TA
recommendation	[ˌrekəmen'deɪʃn]	n. 推荐；建议	U7TA
refine	[rɪ'faɪn]	v. 精炼，改善	U5TB
regimen	['redʒɪmən]	n. [医] 养生法；生活规则；政体	U2TA
regional	['riːdʒənl]	adj. 地区的；局部的	U1TA
regulate	['regjuleɪt]	v. 调节；规定	U6TB

relish	['relɪʃ]	v. 盼望，期待；欣赏；品尝	U8TB
remarkable	[rɪ'mɑːrkəbl]	adj. 卓越的；非凡的	U6TA
renovation	[ˌrenə'veɪʃn]	n. 革新	U6TA
replacement	[rɪ'pleɪsmənt]	n. 代替者；更换	U2TB
replica	['replɪkə]	n. 复制品	U4TB
reserve	[rɪ'zɜːrv]	n. 储备，储存；自然保护区	U1TA
revenue	['revənuː]	n. 税收，国家的收入；收益	U1TA
revive	[rɪ'vaɪv]	v. 复兴；复活	U6TA
rivalry	['raɪvlri]	n. 对抗，较劲	U1TB
rookie	['rʊki]	n. 新手，新人	U2TA
rough	[rʌf]	n. 深草区；高低不平的路面	U4TB
scale	[skeɪl]	n. 规模；刻度；等级	U4TB
sectarian	[sek'teriən]	adj. 宗派的	U1TB
session	['seʃn]	n. 会议	U1TA
showcase	['ʃoʊkeɪs]	v. 使展现；在玻璃橱窗陈列	U2TB
skipping	['skɪpɪŋ roʊp]	n. 跳绳	U7TA
sky-hook	[skai-huk]	n. 天钩；大钩手	U2TA
smash	[smæʃ]	v. 粉碎；使破产	U5TA
solely	['soʊlli]	adv. 单独地，唯一地	U3TA
span	[spæn]	v. 跨越；持续	U2TA
spectacular	[spek'tækjələr]	adj. 壮观的，惊人的；公开展示的	U2TB
spectator	['spekteɪtər]	n. 观众；旁观者	U4TB
sphere	[sfɪr]	n. 范围	U5TB
spinach	['spɪnɪtʃ]	n. 菠菜	U7TB
sponsorship	['spɑːnsərʃɪp]	n. 赞助；发起	U1TA
sportsmanship	['spɔːrtsmənʃɪp]	n. 运动风范，体育道德	U1TB
squad	[skwɑːd]	n. 小队；五人组（篮球队的非正式说法）；班	U2TB
squat	[skwɑːt]	v. 蹲，蹲下	U3TB
stadium	['steɪdiəm]	n. 体育场；露天大型运动场	U3TA
standard	['stændərd]	n. 标准；水准	U3TA
statute	['stætʃuːt]	n. 章程；法规，法令；条例	U1TA
stereotype	['steriətaɪp]	n. 成见；刻板印象	U5TA
stimulation	[ˌstɪmju'leɪʃn]	n. 刺激；激励，鼓舞	U5TA

straighten	['streɪtn]	v. 变直	U3TA
strain	[streɪn]	v. 拉紧；竭力	U3TB
stride	[straɪd]	n. 大步；步幅	U3TB
striking	['straɪkɪŋ]	n. 击打	U7TA
summit	['sʌmɪt]	n. 顶点；最高阶层	U4TA
supreme	[suːˈpriːm]	adj. 最高的，至高的；最重要的	U1TA
surpass	[sərˈpæs]	v. 超越；胜过，优于	U2TA
sustain	[səˈsteɪn]	v. 支持；承受，经受；维持；认可	U4TA
swap	[swɑːp]	v. 与……交换；以……作交换	U7TB
swing	[swɪŋ]	v. 摇摆，摆动	U3TB
tee	[tiː]	n. [高尔夫球] 发球的球座；球梯 v. 将（高尔夫球）置于球座	U4TB
theoretical	[ˌθiːəˈretɪkl]	adj. 理论的	U6TB
torso	[ˈtɔːrsoʊ]	n. 躯干	U3TB
tournament	[ˈtʊrnəmənt]	n. 比赛；锦标赛	U1TA
trace	[treɪs]	v. 追溯，追踪	U6TA
traditionalist	[trəˈdɪʃənəlɪst]	n. 传统主义者；因循守旧者	U4TB
trait	[treɪt]	n. 特性，特点；品质	U1TB
tranquil	[ˈtræŋkwɪl]	adj. 平静的；安宁的	U5TB
transition	[trænˈzɪʃn]	n. 转变；过渡	U4TA
triumph	[ˈtraɪʌmf]	n. 胜利，凯旋	U6TA
ultimately	[ˈʌltɪmətli]	adv. 最后；根本；基本上	U7TA
underlying	[ˌʌndərˈlaɪɪŋ]	adj. 潜在的；根本的	U1TB
unparalleled	[ʌnˈpærəleld]	adj. 无比的，无双的	U3TA
unveil	[ˌʌnˈveɪl]	v. 揭开；揭幕	U5TA
variation	[ˌveriˈeɪʃn]	n. 变异，变种	U5TA
vascular	[ˈvæskjələr]	adj. [生物] 血管的	U5TB
venue	[ˈvenjuː]	n. 场所	U8TB
versatility	[ˌvɜːrsəˈtɪləti]	n. 多才多艺；用途广泛	U2TA
vertically	[ˈvɜːrtɪkli]	adv. 垂直地	U3TA
vibrant	[ˈvaɪbrənt]	adj. 振动的；响亮的；充满生气的	U8TB
vigor	[ˈvɪgər]	n. [生物] 活力，精力	U6TB
vigorously	[ˈvɪgərəsli]	adv. 精力旺盛地；活泼地	U3TB

violation	[ˌvaɪəˈleɪʃn]	n. 违反；妨碍	U3TA
vitality	[vaɪˈtæləti]	n. 活力；生命力	U5TB
wacky	[ˈwækɪ]	adj. 乖僻的，古怪的	U4TB
wrap	[ræp]	n. 包裹物；覆盖物	U7TB